BOY MEETS DEPRESSION

BOY MEETS

DEPRESSION

OR LIFE SUCKS AND THEN YOU ~~DIE~~ LIVE

Kevin Breel

HARMONY BOOKS

Published in the United States by Harmony Books, an imprint of the Crown
Publishing Group, a division of Penguin Random House LLC, New York.
www.crownpublishing.com

Harmony Books is a registered trademark, and the Circle colophon is a
trademark of Penguin Random House LLC.

Library of Congress Cataloging-in-Publication Data
Breel, Kevin.
Boy meets depression / Kevin Breel.
pages cm
1. Breel, Kevin—Health. 2. Depression in adolescence—Patients—
Canada—Biography. 3. Parent and teenager—Biography. 4. Depressed
persons—Family relationships. I. Title.
RJ506.D4B73 2015
616.85'270092—dc23
[B]
2015004695

ISBN 978-0-553-41837-8
eBook ISBN 978-0-553-41838-5

Printed in the United States of America

Jacket design by Jessie Bright

10 9 8 7 6 5 4 3 2 1

First Edition

To the reader: may my story meet you
somewhere in the middle of yours.

Contents

Introduction

MEMOIRS ARE AN interesting, imperfect sort of thing. I always used to wonder who these people were who wrote about themselves, and why they would ever want to do such a thing. From the outside, it looks impossibly selfish. Yet from the inside, it's a bit like pulling your heart out of your chest and gluing it to paper. Plus, when you grab the shovel to start digging up yesterday, you notice that maybe the weirdest part about life is how little of it we actually remember or remember clearly. Seconds turn to minutes and minutes to hours and hours to days, and before long, life has slipped right through your fingers. Trying to go back to the most meaningful moments of our lives, we see just how much has been fractured by memory and the abandonment of time. Writing this book was not unlike being in a river of my weirdest quirks, wondering if at some point that river would meet the sea and I would drown in the disgust and despair of the days that led up to this one. My childhood and teenage years now seem as though they didn't really happen to me. But I know they did, and when I take long enough to get lost in them all over again, I can feel them all the same. It's as if the pain of the past is able to transcend time and healing and show up right back in my heart; uninvited and unwelcome.

Jumping back in and looking at the scenes of my child-hood from different camera angles, I felt at times like I was putting together a ten-thousand-piece puzzle without knowing what the final image was supposed to be. But then as each tiny piece fell into its place, I became more and more aware that my life had been carved out of un-certainity and dragged through darkness. And all of those moments—each tiny and individual, just like yours—come together and become a collective. That collective is this book.

Writing this book was like illuminating every path in my life that has led me to pain and then running up and down and then in circles until I got exhausted. Because the truth is that the past is never really dead. We might think it is, that it's been hidden for so long that it is surely bur-ied. But it is not. It is always just hanging around, waiting for us, practicing the ways in which it will dig back into our lives. While you can distance yourself, you can never fully disown the experiences behind you. Maybe the real truth is: there is no escaping, only acceptance.

This story is a bit like a broken mirror—jagged, painful, with every piece holding up a reflection. If you see yourself in that reflection, then welcome to the club.

I hope this story makes you feel something that maybe you haven't felt for a while. And if you happen to be a kid like me, growing up in a misery that seems like it will never end: I understand you. I get it. And it's all going to be okay. Trust me. I used to be the kid who thought his life was never going to be good or mean anything. Every day I felt like I had my face pressed up against the glass of perfection, watching everybody in the world live a life that was poetic and pure while I drowned in my problems. And I hated it. I used to think that my life, the one I desperately wanted, not the one I had, was never going to show up; that it would always escape me and I would spend my entire existence searching for something that would go unfound.

I used to think that maybe life wasn't really worth much. But that was before any of this happened.

BOY MEETS DEPRESSION

1

The Little House on Hobbs Street

RECENTLY, I FOUND out I had colic as a baby. I don't know exactly what this means other than that my mum says it made me cry a lot and I was fairly unbearable. She said one time she had me in a stroller and an older woman from the neighborhood asked if she could peek inside to see me. When she did, I erupted with noises so vile, I almost gave the poor lady a heart attack. So I came into the world kicking, screaming, and crying. And maybe not much has changed since.

I was a bit of an explosion of a child. Small, with slender shoulders and legs that seemed skinnier than my wrists. My hair was long and moplike, usually flopping over my eyes like a crappy, blond curtain. I was quiet and then devastatingly loud. My eyes were far too big for my face and usually found their way toward the floor until

I knew for sure that you liked me. I was easily hurt and maybe the most sensitive soul my gender has seen in years, which worked against me in almost every way imaginable. On an average day, I was wearing shorts long enough to cover my kneecaps, a T-shirt, and running shoes with laces double knotted so tight it looked like they were swelling up my ankles. It was as if my whole wardrobe had been constructed with the belief that it was far more important to be prepared for impromptu athletic activity than it was to be socially accepted.

I was also thoughtful. When it was my friends' birthdays, I would write them cards. I wrote one friend a poem once. If I went over to someone's house, I always let them win at whatever it was we played. Good sportsmanship and all that. I was an uncertain kid, eager to impress and be loved. I navigated the world with an open heart that, unbeknown to me, was going to be Velcro to the bad stuff and Teflon to the good. Pretty early on, I thought I was very weird. It was a quiet, personal belief that I dared not share with anyone for fear they might put me under a bright light and say, "Aha! You *are* socially and emotionally deformed!"

But somewhere, lurking in the shadows of my juvenile behavior, there were some early-warning signs to confirm my belief that I was a bit defective. I would hump the carpet in my bedroom. I stole a fridge magnet from my mum's friend's fridge—a pink salmon, no less—denied it, hid it, then admitted to it only to still refuse to return it.

If I didn't like the lunch that was packed for me, I would leave it in the bottom of my backpack and let life sort it out. The way life usually sorted it out was by that sandwich going so moldy it was literally a liquid. Until you've opened your Tupperware lunch container and had the liquid mold of a tuna fish sandwich slither down your hand, you haven't really seen just how disgusting bad decisions can turn out.

From the outside looking in, you would never have known that I harbored such an unyielding and horrible self-hatred. Because while in private I was painfully embarrassed about anything and everything that had to do with my own existence, to the rest of the world I was a cocktail of wild, whimsical, and crazy—the first to talk, the first to laugh, and the last to say anything mean. It was as if my personality had been carefully crafted to fill the holes of other kids who were just as broken as I was. I was quick with my tongue, clever with my thoughts, and reckless with my love. I hated myself, and yet no one would have known it. I wanted nothing more than to be accepted. Yet I was determined to do so from a distance, never letting anyone deep enough into my stuff to see just how fucked up it really was.

I GREW UP on a small island on the west coast of Canada. The city I live in is the capital of the province of British

Columbia, but basically no one knows that. Seriously. People who live in Victoria don't even know that. Vancouver is the big, fun city where they host Olympics and good-looking people buy good-looking houses and drive cars that belong on magazine covers, so everyone just assumes Vancouver is the capital. But it's not. Victoria is.

No one has a Ferrari in Victoria. It's a town mainly consisting of elderly people who have come here to retire, play golf, and then pass on peacefully in their bed. It doesn't get too hot in Victoria, and it doesn't get very cold. We usually see snow no more than one day of the year, and the rain is as miserable as it will ever be for the other 364. It's a coastal climate with ocean views and enough old people to sell out a Neil Diamond concert. For a kid, it's a great place to grow up. It's safe and suburban and smells like sea salt. People are kind but not the type of kind that gets annoying after a while with pandering questions and trivial small talk. It's more of a gentle kindness, one that holds sincerity in one hand and brevity in the other. Many people smoke pot and lie by the water and want to experience a life outside of the shuffle of sidewalks and suits. It's the kind of place where everyone stays out of everyone's way and makes sure they do it with a smile, content to just float through their lives on this tiny rock in the middle of the ocean.

I grew up in a small, old white and brown house on Hobbs Street.

I was always convinced the street was named after *Cal-*

vin and Hobbes, and so it was illogical to me that the next streets over weren't named accordingly. I always thought that was the missing piece that really could have pulled the community together. My mum told me when I was about ten that the Hobbes of *Calvin and Hobbes* is spelled with an *e.* I was a teeny bit devastated and yet still equally convinced.

The neighborhood itself was called Cadboro Bay. It had parks and playgrounds and, most important, a basketball court. I spent days as a toddler taking my tiny basketball to the court and heaving it toward the rim, ever hopeful that today would be the day my weak, stringy arms finally launched the ball toward the clouds and then down through the soft mesh. I never even hit the rim. This did little to discourage me.

From the front door of my house to the front door of my elementary school makes 118 steps. I know because I spent a week counting it once. Everything a kid could need was in walking distance of my bedroom. The world seemed like a small and friendly place on Hobbs Street. People knew one another and smiled and had dogs and drove Volvos. Well, we didn't drive a Volvo, but everyone else did. Everything seemed like it was in order. But not in our house. Within the four walls I called home, things were a whole lot different. They were messy and flawed and divorced from the clichéd sense of suburban perfection everyone else seemed eager to portray.

Sometimes I wondered if all families were like that on

the surface, seemingly "normal" (if such a thing exists) and ordered but, behind closed doors, as messy as my own. I thought that would be a fascinating paradox, everyone walking around pretending to be these positive, proper, put-together people but really being just as dysfunctional as us. I know now that's a little true; that there is no perfect family, no normal life. Everyone stumbles through it all the same; the main difference lies not in the lack of dysfunction but in the desire to be dishonest about it. Every family has problems, but only some let you see them. The rest just keep their chaos behind closed doors and out of conversation.

Our house had four massive windows in the front. There was a dying, withering tree in the yard, with our house address halfheartedly hammered into it, but it didn't really obstruct your vision. So basically, if the blinds were open, you could see right into my house. From the first day I was old enough to be aware of it, that always bothered me. I'm not sure exactly why. It just made me feel like we were living in a box, and anyone who wanted to look into our box just had to walk in front of it. It made me feel exposed and naked and vulnerable. More than anything, it made me scared that maybe our personalities were like houses too, and mine had big windows on the front that let anyone who cared to look see just how freaked out and fearful I was about everything.

The number 11 bus drove past about ten to twenty

times a day and shook the walls so violently that one time when I was home alone a framed picture came off the wall and the glass shattered. We had two levels, four bedrooms, an ugly basement, and a beautiful golden retriever named Summer. She was a majestic dog who had a flowing mane and a seriously subdued sense of energy. She spent at least 80 percent of her day lying lazily on the green leather couch in the living room, doing a great job standing guard against any dangerous intruders who might be invading from the sidewalk. When Mrs. Hepple, a woman in her sixties who lived two doors down, walked by on her way to the grocery store, Summer would rise onto all fours and bark so intensely that she would fog up the window pane. The guy who delivered our newspaper once left a note under the doormat saying that we should really train our dog "not to be so angry." I read it and promptly placed it in the trash, partly because I always thought our newspaper delivery guy was a weirdo for wearing a chain wallet and partly because I thought Summer should be as angry or not angry as she wanted. You know, even a dog should have freedom of speech and whatnot. Plus, I could empathize with her situation. I mean, every day we all left on what she probably thought was a never-ending adventure of wonder and awe, and she just stayed on the couch, waiting for one of us to come home and give her love and take her into the big world that she so patiently watched each day from the window.

Barking aside, she was truly a lovely dog. Sadly, she hated me.

Well, *hate* is a strong word. She had a serious dislike for me. I'm not quite sure how that started or where it came from or why I didn't do anything to fix it. I just know that she was deeply convinced that as far as the familial food chain went, she was higher up than I was.

Once, when I was about ten, I started wrestling with her. Summer had two types of growls: a playful growl and a serious growl. To the untrained ear, they might have been indistinguishable. But I could always tell whether she was being playful or getting ready to inflict pain. Or at least I thought I could. So we were wrestling and she was talking to me in her "playful" growl and everything was fine—until in one smooth movement she managed to take an arm of my sweater and wind it around my body, leaving me entangled inside of my own shirt, being dragged around the house by a dog. She just kept pulling on the arm of my sweater, and she did it with such strength that I couldn't recover enough to untangle myself. I wish I was making this up. I had to call for help, and eventually the situation got resolved with a bruised arm and some bruised pride. The thing that always stuck with me was how she didn't hurt me or even want to hurt me. She just wanted to show me what she was capable of. Deep down, it scared the shit out of me that someone's darkness could be disguised like that, that you could go from happy to hurtful in a matter of moments. She was just a dog, but it felt like she was showing me that the sharp edges of life are sometimes hiding just below the surface.

So, we had a house. We had a tree in the front yard. And we had a golden retriever. From the outside, everything seemed right in the world.

But inside of that house, a lot was not so right.

For starters, my mum and dad lived on separate floors. My mum slept in the master bedroom, and my dad slept in the basement suite, which had been somewhat recently renovated and which he had since redecorated with empty beer cans and cigarette butts.

My sister lived in the basement too, but finding her at home was not unlike standing under the sky looking for a shooting star; if you blinked, you'd miss it. She was in a long-term relationship with a boyfriend who had a car and in a short-term relationship with the rest of us. She was awesome and cooler than I could ever give her credit for—to her face, at least—but she came home only to knock off some homework assignments, shower, eat, and tell me my hair looked stupid.

So that left me alone a lot to do whatever I really wanted to do, without much interference or supervision.

I started coming home to an empty house when I was about six. The walk was short, 118 steps, and void of anyone dangerous, so I was allowed to go it alone as soon as I was out of kindergarten. I would usually just saunter home and then lie down somewhere. Sometimes I would give Summer a treat in hopes of bribing her to love me, but usually that love lasted about as long as it took to chew the treat, and then I was at ground zero all over again.

The days were long and lifeless alone in that house. They were lonely, too. To pass the time I learned to daydream. I would make up stories in my head about all kinds of things—what it would be like to be able to fly or walk up the walls or kiss a girl. Sometimes I wondered what it would be like to live life in a different house. A house that had different rules and a dog that liked me and parents who slept on the same floor. Sometimes when I got really deep down the road of unfiltered fantasy, this idea of a new house—one that was impressive and immaculate and beamed importance—would make me smile. Other times I would remember that if I did live in another house, I would probably be forced to do chores. And I hated chores. So I could usually find some contentment in knowing that even though I was caught in the middle of a whole bunch of dysfunction, at least I didn't have to do the dishes. And that always made me feel a bit better.

I always wanted my family to be close. That's probably pretty natural. You want the people you love to all love one another. But in a way, I think I always knew it wasn't possible. My mum had more or less given up on my dad, and my dad had fully committed to giving up on himself. The family glue that is unconditional love had long ago been eroded by chaos and contempt.

. . .

MY PARENTS' RELATIONSHIP made very little sense to me for a variety of reasons, the main one being that I had never seen them act as if they were in love. To me, they were just two people who owned things together. The things they owned everyone could see just from standing out on the sidewalk, looking in through those four big windows. Sadly, what they saw never told the full story.

Because while you could see past the yard with slightly overgrown grass into our house—the living room, the dining room—you couldn't see into our problems. They were pushed down, just beneath the surface, swimming somewhere underneath the disguise of domestication. It was as if our lives were both public and private, in each way equally painful and problematic. I hated what the world knew about us just from looking in—that our TV was old and our couch was ripped and our walls were cluttered with crooked frames. But more than that, I hated what the world did not know about us—that my parents fought and that my sister was never home and that I was all alone.

I knew my family was complicated and broken by the time I was five years old. It didn't take a genius, I suppose.

My mother is a kind woman with warm eyes, a gentle soul, and the ability to listen to you talk about your own bullshit and still be present for hours. Her smile is soft and inviting; she never judges anyone. My dad is a beaten, weathered man who has spent too much time around paint cans and cigarettes to ever look healthy again. He's an alcoholic by every definition of the word and a joyless person by the same definition. He's not a bad man. Not at all. He's just not a happy one.

My sister is a striking, tall feminist with an attitude. She's the type of girl to take a shot of tequila, quote Mother Teresa, and then tell you why you're a misogynist. She's quite fun and has much better taste in music than she does in men.

I learned fairly quickly that my dad and mum didn't love each other. I'm sure at one point they did. They had gotten married, and they look pretty happy in the photos. Then again, they were in Hawaii, and I think I would be pretty happy in Hawaii, too, even if I was losing most of my freedom.

The real reason I knew they didn't love each other, though, was because of how they talked to each other. They weren't yellers or the kind of couple that throw plates at each other's heads. They were both too polite and in-troverted for that. It's just that the way they would talk to each other when they argued was painful, as if the other person's emotional well-being was unimportant, nothing more than a hypothetical concept. It wasn't that they were mean or cruel precisely; it was just that they didn't really care. They were angry and yet indifferent. They didn't ever apologize for what they said or try to empathize with each other. They just sort of shot arrows and walked away before they could find out where they'd landed.

My dad is great at two things in life: fishing and drinking beer. I think in a perfect world he would be living in a cabin in the middle of the woods, living off the land and his bare hands. But life is imperfect and he lived in a city, so he usually resorted to his latter talent to make it through the days. He was a painter by profession and a drinker by passion. Somehow, he still woke up early almost every day. Early to bed, early to rise, I suppose. And he was in bed early, or rather on the couch. Often I would come home from school at three and he would already be passed out on the sofa, a plethora of empty cans lying on the ground for company and his obnoxious snoring as the soundtrack. I was too young to know that those cans littered around his unconscious body had anything to do with his afternoon slumbers, and so I just adopted the assumption that adults needed a lot of naps.

By the time I was old enough to retain memories, my mum and dad were sleeping on separate floors of the house. My knowledge of marriage was limited, but when I went to my friends' houses, usually their parents held hands, kissed or hugged each other, and shared a room. As far as that checklist goes, my parents were 0 for 4.

When my friend Alexandra's parents got divorced, I remember asking her when you know your parents are going to get divorced. She paused and then said, "When they start yelling a lot." I asked her if her parents ever slept in separate rooms. She said they had. I asked her if this was before or after the yelling. She said before. I was no genius, but it seemed like my parents' marriage was headed to an undesirable destination.

There's something indescribably horrible about being a kid in the middle of a broken relationship. You can never feel fully at peace. It's as if the problems of your parents are always right at your feet, waiting for you to trip and fall on them. In one way, it has nothing to do with you. You didn't choose this life. You didn't force these two people to be together. You didn't even recommend they start dating, let alone get married. You don't even know what their problems are, much less how to solve them. But you really want them to love each other. They *should* love each other. I mean, they created little human beings together. That's how I'm alive and my sister is alive—how you're alive—because at one time our parents were so passionate about each other, they thought they should make tiny people together. They couldn't have hated each other then, in that moment. And they certainly couldn't have been in separate rooms then because, even as a young, dumb kid, I knew you couldn't conceive a baby on separate floors. I didn't know much. But I knew that.

When your parents' marriage starts to fall apart, you get a little bit angry at them for it.

At least I did.

My sister, Julena, was four years older than me and therefore four times less likely to talk to me about anything. By the time my parents really started to have their differences, she was barely home anyway. I felt sometimes like she was abandoning me, but I also understood it. I wouldn't be at our house if I didn't have to be. She didn't have to and so she wasn't.

AFTER A WHILE, it seemed to me like most of our family's problems came back to my dad. Every boy wants his father to be the hero of the house, and my dad was something of the opposite.

He's a kind person, I think. He speaks softly and almost never raises his voice in anger or excitement. My father is a tall man, over six feet, but not intimidating. He has big hands and slender shoulders and a closet full of stained shirts. His gray hair is long and wavy, and he has a half-beard, half-mustache thing going on. His hair and scruff never seem to get any longer or shorter; they just sort of exist. Nothing about his appearance seems to change, much like him. Mostly, regardless of setting or circumstance, he seems to be withdrawn, even when he's engaged.

When I was four or five, I can remember him going out to our deck to put strange things in his mouth and then light them on fire. I wouldn't figure out what a cigarette was until years later, but I knew then just by his body language that he was doing something that he wasn't proud of. His shoulders would slide inward and his back would arch slightly upward; his coughs were dry and harsh. But my dad is a good man with a good heart who seems determined to try not to live up to either of those two things.

I have often thought that he is the first person I ever saw who was truly, deeply sad. Anyone can get sad during the right moment, I think. A breakup. A sentimental song. A memory. But my dad was the first person I ever met who could be sad when things were actually good. He would never tell you he was sad with his words, only with his eyes. My mum said he was depressed. I didn't know what that meant, but it sounded serious. Despite any and all concern, he avoided counselors, rejected medication, and embraced his lackluster life, and with each passing day it became less of a song of sadness and more a symphony of self-loathing.

By the time I could string words into sentences, I had written him three letters asking him to stop drinking. He read them all and never changed. Each day the same: passed out on our beat-up green couch, beer can in one hand and what I can only imagine to be regret in the other. When he was awake, he barely talked or had his eyes more than half open. Often he just seemed sort of empty. Like a shell of someone that only he knew, because he was too afraid to show himself to you. I hated him when he was like that. You would say something to him, and he wouldn't hear one word. Sometimes he didn't even know you were talking. Once my sister was trying to tell him something about her day and he was drifting off. She got frustrated and shouted at him, "DAD! Are you sick or something?" He told her he was. She asked him if he was going to die, and—in a memory I can only describe as burned into my brain—he stood up, looked her in the eyes, and said, "You would like that, wouldn't you?" Growing up, his personality, or lack thereof, was a painful thing to be a part of, child from, and witness to each day.

In a lot of ways, I still have no idea who my dad really is. So many people from his past have described him to me as an outgoing, funny person, someone who was full of love and limitless energy. I've never met that person, though. It's not that I don't believe that somewhere deep down inside him this other person exists; it's just that I've seen no evidence of it. It's hard to be convinced of something you can't prove. But some things in life are like that; you can't prove them and you just have to go on believing anyway. I never could, though, with my dad. Mainly because I could never imagine him any other way. I just experienced him as a shell of a man who had lost the spirit of himself and the world around him, and didn't know how to find it again.

He is definitely a smart guy, though. My dad is truly the only guy who if he got stranded on an island somewhere, I wouldn't worry about. He would probably be in his element. One time he went out on the water and his boat got taken by a strong tide and he went missing for a night. No one in my family ever once thought he was dead. We all joked that he was probably having the time of his life. Turns out he ended up on some beach and made a fire and found food and was totally fine. So he is definitely an intelligent, independent man. But he let his own messy mind trick him out of a great life.

Eventually you figure out that when someone stops caring about himself, it becomes really hard for that person to keep on growing and living or loving. The worst part about it for me was that despite all this, I really did want to love him and be loved by him, and that made me both strong and weak at the same time.

Every day was a long day in that house on Hobbs. Cars passed by, but the hours never seemed to. It was like living inside of a dream; watching the whole world pass by as I stood still. I loved my mum very much, and when my sister would let me, I loved her a lot too. But I never really enjoyed being in that house. It was small, cluttered, and chaotic. I wanted to be outside with the rest of the world, doing all the fun things I was constantly witnessing other people doing. I wanted to have friends and do things with them. I wanted to grow up and get out of that house. The trouble with being a kid, though, is that getting out of the house means going to school.

When my mum first told me that I'd be starting school soon, I was curious. I knew very little about what school was other than it was where everyone spent a lot of their time. My sister—four years older and, to my mind, having four times the fun—brought home stories of school, ones that seemed impressive: like how she got to go hiking or hold a dead frog. It sounded like a whirlwind of adventure, alive with new people and possibilities. And even if it wasn't, it was still going to get me out of my house. I couldn't wait.

What was I thinking?

NOTE TO SELF

No one's family is perfect. No one's life is perfect. Never trust anyone who wears a chain wallet.

2

Boredom and Bullies

THERE IS NOBODY more socially awkward than Ben. Granted, when we first met he could hardly speak English. But his social awkwardness wasn't just in what he said but in how. He would ask you a question and then right as you made eye contact to answer him, he would use his palm as a Kleenex and smear snot all over the inside of his hands. While. Maintaining. Eye. Contact. Admittedly, at this point in my young life, I had never experienced any foreign cultures, but I assumed there was no place on earth where this was customary. Max was different. Max was not yet tall, but you could tell he was going to be. His hands were comedically oversized—like someone had put two baseball gloves on an infant—and his arms dangled down to his knees. He was kind in a quiet, fearful sort of way and he would fake injuries as if his deepest passion in life was to be in theater. If he stumbled or slid on the playground, he would curl into a ball. When you got close enough to ask him if he was okay, he would emit these irregular noises. It was him pretending to cry. You would have to give him a couple minutes to revel in it before he would stand back up, looking proud and defiant to have overcome such devastation. These were my first classmates, at least the ones that now stick out in my mind.

My school was down a long, poorly paved path, decorated with the occasional crevice or bump to give it character. From the start of the path, if you squinted really, really hard, you could just see where the school's walls poked out and the bike rack stood. That building was my elementary school, a small establishment that was home to about five hundred kids at any given time. As far as schools went, it was not a bad one. I only had one problem with school: I hated it.

It wasn't so much the school itself. I was fairly neutral to the pastel-colored walls and chalkboards and the old, beat-up floors that smelled like wood. It was more what school represented, and that I felt sick to my stomach almost every night thinking about having to go. I hated the long hours and how they made my days feel devoid of any optimism. I hated the suffocating sense of routine. I hated the cramped classrooms that smelled like cleaning supplies and those stupid single-pane windows that did little other than offer a view to a world we were not allowed to explore. The desks that were all too small and rotting and had curse words carved into them—the physical proof of mind-numbing boredom. I was convinced that there was not a single thing worthwhile there, that it was nothing more than an empty shell someone had already scraped all the joy out of.

Day after day, my eyes would dance upward, staring up at the big clock at the top of the wall, as I hoped that somehow time had leapfrogged forward since I'd last been brave enough to look. Habitually, I counted down the hours until I would be handed back my freedom. While at first school had seemed to promise a social circle to become entrenched in, I was quickly realizing it was less of a social club and more of a detention center. I had once craved the escape from my quiet house, and now I craved nothing more than to be in my bedroom, able to get lost in fantasy and daydream without disruption. Most of my friends felt the same way. Or at least they said they did. But I always wondered whether they meant it the way I meant it. When I said I hated school, I meant it the way a guy in the desert says he needs water. When they said they hated school, they said it the way a horny guy says he loves a girl when he knows she needs to hear that to take her clothes off. Granted, they were all just as miserable as me or any other mope when we were learning math or doing one of those lame-ass craft projects where you glue Popsicle sticks to a piece of paper and then paint them. But they seemed easily swayed by a short recess and the occasional snack. I didn't care for kickball, and I didn't want a juice box. I wanted to be doing the things I wanted to do. And school wasn't what I wanted to do. Truthfully, I didn't even know what it was I did want to do, but I knew it wasn't this. It definitely wasn't this.

This was the first time in my life that my fantasies collided head-on with my reality. The whole idea of doing what you have to do instead of what you want to do is an outrageous concept for a kid. Before you are old enough to go to school, if you want something, you can basically just point at it and get it, or scream incoherently when you don't. Whether out of eternal love or the need to guard against eardrum damage, eventually someone will give you what you want or tell you to shut up. Because you're a kid. And kids' lives are supposed to be one big fantasy land of limitless possibility. But this business of having to "do what we're supposed to do" or do something just because others tell us to seemed like a load of crap. Truthfully, it left a very bitter taste in my mouth. Everyone talked about how going to school is "the right thing to do," yet I just kept wondering why, if that was true, school felt so devastatingly wrong.

I became very militant in my questioning about the logic behind school. Weekly, I would bother my mum about why we had to go to school. I'd ask her, with all the seriousness a six-year-old can muster, who invented it. She said that no one "invented" school, that the government had created it as an infrastructure to help promote the education of children to become high-functioning adults and productive people. I took a little time to digest this, and then I asked her how I could get in touch with this "government" she spoke of. She never gave me a straight answer to that question, and that always bothered me. It didn't much matter though. My mind was made up: whoever was behind this school thing might have designed its infrastructure for kids, but they sure didn't care much about their happiness.

OUTSIDE OF YOUR family, school is often the first time many kids have to seriously interact with adults. You don't know them and they don't know you, but there are built-in rules and expectations. Some kids try to duck and dodge their way around it, but ultimately you have to please the teachers if you want to make it through. They are the gatekeepers to your eventual release. Part of the reason I think that I never fell in love with school was because I never really fell in love with any of my teachers. Most of them seemed bitter and angry, like they had been sitting in the same chair, at the same desk, in the same room, for far too long. I just couldn't quite grasp the concept of wanting to be a teacher. The idea that anyone could endure a childhood of classrooms, then spend his or her early adulthood in a larger classroom, only to return after, shocked me. I hated school.

The most memorable teacher I ever had was a guy who I'll call Mr. Moss. Sadly, he was memorable for all the wrong reasons. Often, his temper would escape him and he would erupt at his students in fiery outbursts of profanity. He had an almost Afro, or as close as you could get if you're a forty-year-old white guy, and he always made sure his polo was tucked into his track pants. Every single day for three years, he stayed true to this uniform, unwilling to conform in the name of societal norms or personal hygiene.

To this day, I've never met anyone whose job is to work with kids who hated kids as much as Mr. Moss did. It was almost as if he had lost a bet and had to become a teacher, his buddies forcing him to follow through and do it. His raging disdain for the average kid in his classroom was so palpable it was practically coming through his teeth. Once, let's call him Michael Smith, a shy blond kid who sat in the corner of class and sometimes put his hand down his pants, had his watch alarm accidentally go off. It was a cheap watch and the face of it couldn't have been bigger than a nickel, but the thing had a serious sound system on it. It was blaring so loudly, it reminded me of the fire drills where they insist on blaring the alarm just to prove a point. So his watch starts going off, and needless to say, it wasn't exactly increasing productivity within the classroom. He didn't know how to shut it off. Or at least he didn't know how to shut it off in high-pressure social situations. Whatever the reason, Mr. Moss wasn't in the mood for it. The watch just kept beeping loudly and people were laughing and Michael was panicking. Initially just irritated, Mr. Moss was now irate.

"Bring that damn watch up here!"

Sheepishly, Michael rose from his desk and shuffled toward the front, awkwardly transferring his watch from his wrist to his palm. Mr. Moss grabbed it out of his hands forcefully and placed it on a desk in front of everyone in the class. For a minute, he just stared at it silently. Then he stood up, walked to the back of the room, opened the door to the makeshift supply closet that doubled as a place to put our coats, and came back holding what looked like a small bowling ball. It turned out it was a shot-put ball, the kind they make guys who can lift cars throw in the Olympics because they're so heavy. He went back to the front of the room and then smashed the watch into a million pieces. Everyone in the room grew silent, as if we had all just witnessed a small puppy get hit by a bus. I looked over at Michael, and he had the strangest look on his face, as if he had seen something that made him really happy and really sad at the same time. I had to admit, there was a strange sensation of tranquillity in having that beeping go silent. Still, no one knew what to do afterward. But it was clear from that point on that Mr. Moss was one part teacher, three parts ticking time bomb. If school is all about learning, my biggest takeaway thus far was that the social scenery around me was shaky, scary, and unpredictable.

THE OTHER THING about school that can go wrong is the kids.

Some kids end up getting bullied. There's not much way around it. Some kids just get picked on and made fun of, and other kids don't. I'm not sure why. I just know it happens. I was one of those kids who got bullied.

No one really gets bullied because they "deserve" it. At least, I don't think so. It's hard to imagine how a kid could possibly deserve a life sentence of social torture. But if I had to guess why I got bullied, I would probably blame my looks. I wasn't necessarily an ugly kid. *Ugly* is a strong word. I just had a face that was relatively punchable. I can say this objectively and without much self-judgment because I've taken the time to really think about it. I had floppy hair with curls and looked afraid of physical contact, and those factors seemed to hold great appeal to the basic elementary school bully in my hometown.

Plus, I was really sensitive. Grossly, embarrassingly, sensitive. The kind of sensitive that reeks off of you, like a smoke signal of insecurity. Maybe that came from growing up in a dysfunctional home or watching too many movies with my mother, or maybe I was just a "total pussy," as it was once described to me. I'm not exactly sure why I was so sensitive. I just know it was who I was. I was emotional and seemingly had a broken Stop button on my tear ducts. Literally. As a baby, I cried so much that my mum took me to the doctor and found out that one of my tear ducts, which is basically the thing that holds in your tears, wasn't working. I had to get surgery for it. Bizarre.

So it was pretty simple to get a reaction out of me. I cried easily and I was too kind—or too uncertain—to really care to defend myself. My own gentle nature became something of a gateway to getting my ass kicked. Everything a bully is looking for in a potential victim could be found in me. So I got bullied. It started out small, the way things like this do. At first, it was just a group of kids, Hayden, Alex, and Kelly, who were mean to me. Mostly verbal jabs, like "Breel likes to kneel!" with an obligatory sucking-of-penis motion with their mouths, and the occasional trip in the hallway. They would say things about how I shot a basketball like a girl and how I sucked on the drawstrings of my sweaters, which, much to my disdain, was actually true. I sucked on my strings when I was nervous, and I knew it was every bit as embarrassing as it sounded, but I really couldn't stop. There's something relaxing about it, I guess. So these guys would make comments about all of my quirky habits, and they were a year older and not so nice, and I was insecure, so I just allowed it to happen.

It's worth saying that individually all three of them were okay guys. Together, though, they morphed into some sort of wannabe prepubescent playground gang determined to keep themselves entertained through my discomfort and that of others. The ironic thing is, everyone talked nonstop about bullying at my school. There were posters all over the hallways about bullying and little signs in the bathroom that had a drawing of a kid pushing another kid into what looked like a trash can, with a big red X through it. Someone even came to our school to give a speech about bullying. She talked for the better part of an hour, enough time to send a kid into the deepest boredom, but I remember that she was a pretty good speaker. She told us stories of how the bullies at her high school used to order pizzas to be sent to her house and fill up her backpack with lima beans. All that stuff sounded original and almost funny. Disappointingly, my situation was nothing like that. There was no planning or preparation. These guys preferred to inflict pain improvisationally, as if that somehow made it more impressive. What they lacked in cleverness, they made up for in cruelty. There was no wordplay or innuendos, just good old-fashioned meanness.

One of their favorite things to do was to "waterfall" me. If you're unacquainted with such maturity, a waterfall is when you're innocently standing somewhere and someone comes up behind you and kneels down right below your kneecaps, and then someone else runs at you from the front and pushes you over the person who, unbeknownst to you, has been kneeling behind you the whole time. The entire operation takes about ten seconds and should leave you with no less than two bruised ribs. Anything less than injury or tears means they didn't try hard enough. Hayden, Alex, and Kelly did this to me about once a week for a year straight. Over time I became less reactive to the waterfall. I figured out how to see one coming, and they became pretty avoidable. Plus I learned that even if you do get blindsided, all you need to do is pull your heels up as you feel yourself going down, thus introducing your shoes to the face of the guy kneeling behind you. Turns out if you do this once or twice, no one wants to be the guy who kneels anymore. This was a valuable lesson for me— that sometimes people do things to you because they don't know how bad it feels to have those things done to them.

SCHOOL IS JUST hard. It's this big social experiment of all these different people being in a close, prisonlike atmosphere and trying to all get along. It's bound to be bad news. And if it's not bad news, at the very least it's boring. You walk through the big doors into the big box and then walk through a smaller door into a smaller box, and then you sit at your little box desk and wait for someone to tell you it's okay to eat your box lunch. The whole thing starts to feel like one long, drawn-out study to see just how far you can push kids before they snap. I guess the thing they don't account for is that often the kids and the teachers all snap on one another.

It's hard to be young and have people be mean to you. No one really ever tells you how to deal with that. I assumed that the best way was to ignore it. I didn't want to talk about it or even think about it really. But dealing with it—fighting back or telling your folks or any of that—that isn't the hard part. Not really. The hard part is trying to figure out whether or not those people are right about you. If enough people tell you something with enough conviction, it's pretty easy to believe it. I felt like every day I was getting told with piercing and convincing clarity that I was dull and dumb and didn't matter too much to anyone. After a while, I guess I started to wonder if that was true. I didn't know what to think. I just knew I was lonely and unloved and I hated how that felt.

I became so used to the daily routine of rejection that I almost didn't notice how badly it hurt anymore. I had accepted my place on the social totem pole, and I was too tired to even think about how to change it. Maybe I deserved all the teasing. I was soft, inside and out, and I knew it. My leaky eyes and my skinny legs that made me look like "a torso on top of two pencils" were all just visible evidence of what a loser I was. Perhaps I could have changed it. Maybe I could have figured out how to win over my enemies. My stupid body and my stupid hair and my stupid face had set me up for a lifetime of shame, it seemed like then.

I dared not tell my family about this, either. At first, because I thought that if I told them about my attackers, they might actually agree with them. I had this bubbling, blinding worry that once I told them, they would all stop and go, "Well, now that you mention it . . ." Then, once I got over that thinking, I didn't tell them simply because I didn't want them to know that the kid they had told so often that he was special had finally found out he wasn't. I thought I would be disappointing them, as if their self-worth was tied to my ability to successfully climb the social ladder of elementary school. Fear and secrecy were two habits I adopted early, I guess. So I didn't tell them for a long time. I just kept showing up at school and showing up at home and pretending that both of those places were fantastic. I wondered if maybe, if I made myself think it enough times, it eventually would be true. Pathologically, I continued on this path of quasi self-motivation, each day determined to drill into my head that I was happy.

I guess for me school was something of an intellectual and emotional prison. Inside those walls, my chaotic yet closeted need to fit in and find friends was almost always begging to be let out. The dysfunction inside my house had left me craving the intimacy of true friendship and connection. Even though I wasn't unloved at home, there were parts of me that felt empty. I wanted to win others' affection for no reason better than to prove to myself that I could. Prove that I was lovable. Prove that maybe I wasn't a loser. It's exhausting to be so hard on yourself. Even worse than all of this, though, may be that I thought relief would come in the form of finding people who accepted me. I never knew that the most important thing was breaking down the high walls of self-hatred and actually accepting myself.

ONE DAY I finally reached my breaking point. My scooter—a crappy, cheap, metallic painted thing that was all the rage—got stolen from the school. I knew who did it almost before I knew my scooter was gone. They took it for a joyride and left it just down at the end of the path, close to my house. I walked home that day with tears flowing, cursing my genetics and weak-ass tear ducts.

At home, I told my mum I wanted to switch schools. I was done.

NOTE TO SELF

If no one chooses you, choose yourself. If no one accepts you, accept yourself. And if you wanna suck on your sweater, suck on your sweater and tell everyone else to eat shit.

3

Brother from Another Mother

MY NEW SCHOOL was called Willows. It was a gigantic, old, and looming building that had a stadium-sized soccer field, where my bus stopped each morning. It felt fresh and scary all in one. I showed up on the first day not knowing a single soul, and almost instantly I regretted transferring there. The students already knew one another. Perhaps this should have been obvious. But I had been so desperate to escape my own hurt that I hadn't taken the time to truly think it through. Now it was hitting me right in the face: everyone at Willows—a confusing cocktail of an institution, mixing elementary and middle-school students all together—had been going to school together for the last five years and were already friends, while everyone I knew was still somewhere in Cadboro Bay. Here I was the dreaded new kid, sticking out, reeking of desperation, destined for isolation. I was all alone, hoping that somehow things would change for the better. I would make friends and dance off into the sunset, while sticking my middle finger up to my bullies and big-headed teachers.

AT SOME POINT, and it might as well be now, it's probably worth explaining that I am not very good at friendship.

It's not that I'm bad at it. I'm not an asshole or anything. I just have certain quirks that make it hard for people to like me. I'm fidgety. I have a hard time focusing on other people. I'm selfish. Not like "I think I'm so cool and you can't tell me otherwise" selfish but like "I interrupt your story about your dying dog to tell you a joke that's only funny to me" selfish. I want to go for coffee and talk about women and the economy and other things I know exactly nothing about, but at the same time I don't drink coffee and I hate conversations that rely only on observation. I want to talk to people about real things—fears, dreams, why anyone insists on drinking soy milk—and all the good stuff. I have a very hard time with small talk. I don't want to fake caring about things that seem insignificant to me or that I think are stupid. And maybe that's why it's hard for me to be in friendships with many people at any particular time. But that's the thing; while I hate small talk and pleasantries, I have this deep desire to be friends with almost everyone. I love people. I want to know them and enjoy them. I would like to believe that, as far as human beings go, I'm a decent one who is pretty easy to talk to and nonjudgmental. And with enough social persuasion, I can even close my mouth and listen.

It takes time to develop these friendship things, though. It takes a lot of time. It takes phone calls and long drives at weird hours, and showing up and being present and listening to long stories that sometimes kind of suck. All those things feel more like commitment than freedom. And while I crave friendship, I also crave freedom. I want as few barriers between me and getting lost in my own little world of fantasy as possible. So it seems there is a clashing point between freedom and friendship, between my own unselfish desire to love and my completely selfish desire to have absolutely no obligations, to anyone, under any circumstances.

But maybe all of this—the thoughtfulness, the effort, the excruciating experience of listening to someone tell you a story they've already told you—is the point of friendship. Maybe we're supposed to learn to love, so we can see that there really is a purpose in investing in other people. Maybe we need to care for others before we can appreciate the ways in which others care for us. Maybe we need friendship as a way of forcing us to focus on something other than ourselves.

Every once in a while, though, someone walks into your life whose presence is so compelling, you forget you want freedom. You forget that friendship is supposed to be hard. You forget it could ever be time-consuming or draining or stressful, because it's none of those things. It's like this one person is the perfect version of all your carefully constructed demands about what a person should be in order to be your friend. Sometimes that person just walks straight into your life and changes everything for you.

For me, that person was a kid named Jordan McGregor.

JORDAN BECAME MY best friend the way a good joke builds to the punch line—slow at first and then all at once and unstoppable. He was the shortest kid in school and nearly always wore a soft smile and a puffy jacket. He was never without that jacket, even when it was hot and the world was practically screaming at him to take it off. He lived walking distance from our school, and it became known rather quickly that Jordan's house was what could only be respectfully described as a lawless land. His dad was a pleasant man named Jim who owned his own business and his own time. His company was as unconventional as it gets—a hot dog stand where you could buy a fat-filled corn dog and also rent a vintage car. American tourists loved it; it was as if parading around in an automobile with no seat belts and a screaming muffler was a rite of passage when visiting Canada. Jim had a collection of bizarre and mind-boggling cars: stretch limos long enough for dozens of people and Hummers with hot tubs in the back, and old town cars that looked like presidents from the sixties would have ridden in them.

They were not a rich family—they rented their house and moved every two years or so—but they were a fun family. Jim was one of the coolest dads anyone could ever ask for, and without asking for it, he kind of became my dad, too. Invariably, he wore almost the exact same outfit each day: a devastating combination of stained khaki pants, New Balance running shoes, a polo shirt that was only half tucked in, and a crappy cream-colored hat. It was like he woke up each day determined to give the middle finger to whoever was a fan of fashion or variety.

Most of the time at Jordan's house we were free to do absolutely anything we wanted. This was a dangerous amount of unsupervised time to give prepubescent boys, and we always made the most of it. A crew of us would hang out at Jordan's house and stay up way too late watching horror movies and eating candy. Adam was my friend who had messy hair and six-pack abs. Seriously. He had a real, defined six-pack when we were all still waiting for our dicks to grow. It was the coolest thing in the world, and we showed him that by never, ever speaking of it while he was around. Trent was the first person I ever met who actually made real-life fart jokes. It's some sort of male cliché that we hang out all day talking about poop and piss and sex. Or, at least I thought it was. But then I met Trent, and he opened my eyes to everything unspeakably disgusting. Often, he would parade into the living room and shout, "TIME FOR TRENT TO OPEN HIS VENT!" and release the kind of gas that, if there was enough of it, could claim the life of a small child. Chris McBride would sometimes tag along, too. He was six feet tall before he was ten and looked almost like a cartoon character; his feet pointed inward, his shoulders slumped, and his back hooked like he was trying to touch his chest to his stomach. He was horribly uncoordinated, and I felt terrible for him. The beautiful part about Chris though was that he spun all of this into comedic genius, overamplifying his lack of coordination and constantly taking physical injuries and embarrassment in the name of a good laugh. He was our real-life version of a stunt man, our Jackass. There was nothing he wouldn't do to make us smile.

So that was our crew. And staying up every Friday night at Jordan's, we were convinced that life could get no better. Perhaps we had a point. There were no rules, no responsibilities, no regulations. We just had fun. It was a great way to grow up. I used to tell my mum some of the stuff that would happen at the house, and she would get way worried and tell me that I shouldn't stay up past midnight and that I certainly shouldn't be watching any movies where "people are murdering other people." She said a whole list of other things that I deemed unimportant to listen to. I thought then that adults were all basically jaded kids who didn't want us to have fun anymore because they couldn't have fun themselves. Jim was the only adult I had ever met who still wanted to be a kid. The toys and the fun had just gotten bigger. I thought that was pretty cool.

My friendship with Jordan quickly became the best and healthiest thing in my life. His family embraced me and made me feel like I mattered. There was always so much going on in that house, and it was never quiet or empty or lonely. I always felt like I was a part of something there. In time, it felt easier to be at Jordan's house than it did my own. We did what we wanted, talked like we wanted, and we didn't have to listen to anybody. It was sort of like living in a somewhat-regulated fraternity. And it made my life feel full for the first time ever.

THERE WERE TWO younger kids at Willows who never ceased to be both annoying and worthy of an ass kicking, one that we all freely said they should get but were physically too scared to act upon. Let's call them Nate and Jeff. They were something of a tag team: ridiculous, rude, and borderline behaviorally challenged. Jeff was a little more toned down—he had a buzz cut and was a bit big around the middle and a bit brainless near the top. Nate was the opposite—razor thin, with a bullshit smile and a silver chain that had his name etched into it, as if he had been in 'Nam or something. Nate talked way more shit than Jeff could even process, and that's why they were a wonderful sort of tandem: Nate spurting off at the mouth about things he had no business talking about, and Jeff nodding because he lacked the mental capacity to think of a reason not to. Nate was socially blind and Jeff was intellectually deaf, and together they were one chaotic little couple. All of this was fine and well until Nate started directing his shit talking toward us.

"Heyyyyy, Jordan McGreeeegor! The gap in your teeth is bigger than a craterrrr!" This was one of his more clever, better-constructed bits. Mostly, it was just harmless stuff, hallway heckles or a comment as you left the washroom, but eventually, like a locomotive train determined to run headfirst into a concrete wall and combust, he just kept on bringing his big mouth to us and opening it wide enough to see down his throat and into all the ugly parts of his soul. He really was an asshole, if it's possible for a ten-year-old to be such a thing.

Everything reached a climax one day when Nate and Jeff came out to the basketball court during recess. We were playing a game of full court. It was well known that while our group was playing, our games were not to be interrupted, disturbed, or otherwise interfered with unless someone was seeking death by way of social humiliation.

But Nate came right out and started shooting on the side of the court that we were temporarily not using. When the ball went through the hoop and the game headed back his way, he just kept on shooting. The audacity of this kid poured out of every pore in his body and could reek up a room.

"Hey! You ever heard of something called get the fuck out of here?" Brandon Parmar, an intimidating East Indian kid who already had a chin strap and forty pounds of muscle on him, shouted out. Nate, ever immune to commentary that didn't carefully pat his ego, decided to ignore this. Chris Hartley, well chronicled as both a shit disturber and an enemy of Nate's, took this opportunity to make a cut to the corner, shoving Nate to the ground effortlessly as he did, as if that was how he'd learned to make that cut in the first place. Pissed, Nate stood up and threw his basketball at Chris's head, narrowly missing the glasses that everyone said gave him a striking resemblance to Harry Potter. They said some words to each other, all of which were muffled by the bouncing of the ball and the continuation of our full-court game.

Before I knew what was happening, they were pushing each other, still swearing and saying words that were half grunt, half obscenity. Trying to defuse the situation, we all stopped playing and started the age-old tradition of everyone holding everyone back and yet at the same time shoving the other people trying to hold everyone else back.

It was a good old-fashioned melee of wannabe masculinity. And that's right when everything went wrong.

I grabbed Nate by the shirt and used all my prepubescent muscle definition to move him back a few feet. I guess it must have been the breaking point, because as soon as I moved him, he unleashed a series of sentences that were both so fast and so vulgar, I couldn't process them linearly. It was like I was going through a time travel of insults, bobbing and weaving my way through *fucks, shits*, and *you ugly motherfuckers*. At first they all rolled right off me, like a waterfall of rejected insults. But Nate, being Nate, just had to open his mouth one last time, just in case there was any confusion about whether or not he was clearly the worst person walking the walls of Willows.

"Well, at least my dad isn't a drunk and poor and driving a shitty-ass red truck!"

I heard the words first through my ears and then through my heart. Now, of course, I actually agreed with Nate. My dad was all of those things. He was a drunk, his truck was basically a body of rust on wheels, and my family was far from rich. But I wasn't going to let him know that. I tried to think of something to say, and when my brain went totally blank, I resorted to what any self-respecting kid would do and tried to punch him in the face. Pathetically, the punch never really made it anywhere near his face, as I had telegraphed it so much with my body that about five people had latched on to my shoulders before

I could gather any forward momentum. For a split second you could see a look of pure shock in his eyes as he tried to understand what was happening. For the first time ever, he had gone from smug to scared. Even though no one punched him in the face that day, in a weird way this was much more satisfying. Before I could bask in the glow of everything being right in the world, teachers were all over the court, yanking us off one another, picking up all the basketballs, and quarantining us in separate rooms in the school. They said they were going to call our parents and tell them what had happened. I hoped that when they did, they would tell them that for the first time ever, I had some friends who had my back.

It felt fantastic, as though the sheer joy of it all was piercing through my skin and deep into the unnourished parts of my soul.

THE SUMMER AFTER we finished middle school, everything seemed possible. Puberty-related body insecurity and voice cracks aside, the world was our tiny, unharvested oyster. That summer, none of the hard, awkward stuff seemed to matter at all. Being a teenager was right around the corner. High school would be coming with the wind and the leaves and the fall, and everything was wide open and full of optimism. Jordan even got a girlfriend. I was shocked, then amused, and then just confused. I thought it was cool, but it also kind of annoyed me because it seemed like we hung out less. I was into girls too, but I couldn't imagine having a girlfriend. Whenever I thought about a relationship, all my mind could visualize was an old black-and-white movie scene where a prisoner watches the guard close his cell door. The prisoner desperately begs for mercy, for his freedom, and for his future, "PLEASE! I HAVE A FAMILY!" and then the door slams shut and the room goes all black and he screams. Even at a young age, I was showing all the signs of impressive maturity.

Jordan's girlfriend's name was Kimberly. She had purple hair and a nose ring and had done drugs. I thought she was either a total badass or a freak. After I hung out with her a few times though, I realized she was actually sort of wonderful and I decided I shouldn't be mean to her just because she had a bigger piece of Jordan's heart than I did. Occasionally we even all hung out together as one big group. Chris was too busy tripping over himself to talk, Trent got self-conscious about his fart jokes around girls, and Adam was probably just off somewhere doing sit-ups. So it was usually pretty awkward. Kimberly said she had lots of friends who would love to date me, and I always just assumed that she was either lying or still on drugs. Either way it didn't much matter. I wasn't very interested yet, and it was summer and the sun was out and the world was ours for the first time. Finally, we were old enough to ride the bus and go downtown alone;

this on its own was not unlike a VIP pass to our own personal Narnia.

I had never felt it before, but that summer it seemed as though there was some kind of switching of the guard, where the kids became free and the parents had to work. We were having so much fun. It felt like we were riding the wave of today, and when that wave delivered us to the sandy shore of tomorrow, we were really going to become something. After all, we were going to high school. The promised land. The mecca of all things that mattered. Sure, I had always hated school. But this was *high school*. Not a place of education but rather an invitation to be a badass. The chance to step away from being boys and become men. This was our golden moment: an opportunity to take life by the horns, to fulfill our potential, and to "get a bunch of pussy and shit," as Trent once worded it. Jordan and I were going to share a locker, high-five each other in the hallways, and wear letterman jackets. And nothing—not even our own overly naïve and narrow view of what the whole experience would be—could stop us.

SOMEWHERE NEAR THE middle of July, while summer still retained its strongest sense of optimism, I had to go on a trip with my mum. It worked out well because Jordan had to go on a trip with his mum, too. Our lives seemed to be in sync like that sometimes. His parents had divorced a long time ago, and his mum had become a lesbian. I didn't really know what that meant other than one time I slept over at his mum's house and when I woke up in the morning about twenty women were in the kitchen drinking orange juice and champagne and they gave me a glass. So that was what I thought it meant to be a lesbian: you woke up early and mixed alcohol and fruit juice.

So off we went on road trips with our mums. They promised to be full of boredom and bathroom breaks on the side of ugly highways, and I was walking the line between anger and acceptance about the whole thing. Jordan said that we had to build our go-carts when we got home. I agreed. We had been working on a "great idea" to build two go-carts and drive them around his neighborhood. Considering his neighborhood consisted of mostly retired couples, small families, and one man in a wheelchair, it sounded pretty genius to us. Jim knew how to put the motor in, and so "all we had to do" was build the frame. You know, just a part-carbon-fiber, part-metal frame for a moving vehicle to be constructed from. In hindsight, I don't think either one of us could have built a proper pillow fort, but we were mighty convinced that building the chassis of a small car would be no problem at all. So I went off with my mum and Jordan went off with his mum, and I told him to call me when he got home. He said we had a deal. I remember leaving his garage and kicking myself for not taking a Gatorade from his fridge.

The road trip was about as boring as I had predicted it would be. My mum wouldn't let me listen to any music with swear words, and when you're twelve, the *only* music you want to listen to is music with swear words. Cursing is kind of like a hit of heroin when you're twelve. It's a delicious feeling, and every adult in the world discouraging you from doing it only adds to the magnificence.

We were spending time in the big city, Vancouver, where my mum was catching up with her friend Liz, who alongside being an incredible lady is also incredibly wealthy. Her house looked like it was from one of those home style magazines that they always put on the shelf at grocery stores, the ones always awkwardly squeezed between a gossip magazine and a fringe news magazine with compelling headlines like "Are Aliens Invading Arkansas?!" and "Sources Close to the President Say 'He Can't Stop Sucking His Nipples!'"

Liz's house was hauntingly gorgeous, with a long stretch pool, a hot tub, and a view of what seemed, at the time, like the entire universe. After a few nights there, my mum seemed really happy. Maybe that was just the wine they drank daily, but it didn't much matter to me. I felt happy for her. It felt good to see her happy, and it felt good to be in a big, clean, beautiful house. Even though ours wasn't anything like hers, it felt good to know that people who had things like these didn't think people like us were scum. The room I slept in was off to the side of the house, with a balcony that seemed to stretch out impossibly far and a bathroom that was bigger than my bedroom. I had no idea that everything about my life was going to change while I was hanging out in that room.

Two nights into our trip, I was nestled into a corner, reading a book on how an NBA referee fixed a bunch of games and made millions of dollars before he got caught. I was halfway through it and more underwhelmed than I had imagined I could be when I first opened it up. I turned off the light and stared out the window. The moon was a quarter full, hanging there looking as if someone had used a butter knife to cut a chunk out of it. It shined a hello through the tiny window to the left of my bed, and there was something about it that was oddly comforting. I smelled terrible from playing out in the sun all day, and my eyelids felt like they were being pulled downward by some combination of gravity, boredom, and exhaustion. The blaring red digits on the alarm clock directly in front of the bed told me that it was just after 9:30. As I contemplated whether to step out onto the balcony to look at the moon or just give in to sleep, my mom came in. She said something to me in a low quiet voice that I couldn't quite hear.

Before I could muster up the energy to ask her to repeat herself, I heard the phone ring. It seemed a bit late for a phone call, but it wasn't our house and it wasn't our phone, so I was unbothered by it. No one answered it, so the phone just kept ringing; it seemed to get louder the more it went ignored. That echo filled every inch of the house, and for a little while I couldn't hear anything else. Then everything went silent again. I looked back at my mom, about to open my mouth to speak, and as if on cue, the phone rang once more.

Brinnnnnnnnnnnnng!

Finally, I heard Liz pick up the phone. It was hard to hear, because of both the distance and my lack of interest, but it seemed like she was coming up the stairs. Abruptly, Liz walked into the room, seeming slightly off balance, almost unnerved, and looked over at my mum, holding the phone out toward her, as if it were a possession she had no use for. My mum took it with a mixture of surprise and silence. She started talking, and from the tone of her voice, I knew right away it was my dad. I watched as my mother's eyes got bigger and bigger, her breath coming higher into her chest and her hand closing over her mouth. She maintained her silence for another few seconds, as if she was bracing herself for a punch that she knew she couldn't avoid. Suddenly, the tears started to flow and she handed the phone to me. Thoughts raced in and out of my mind. Rarely, if ever, did I see my mum cry. I tried to think of anything it could be. Our dog? The house? Did she find out about the porn the guys and I had searched on the computer? Before I could entertain anything rooted in logic, I was on the line, hearing my father's heavy breathing vibrate in my ear.

"Hello?"

"Hey, Kev . . ."

"Yeah?"

"I'm so sorry, man. But . . . Jordan . . . Jordan was in a car accident, and Jim just called me to say that he didn't make it."

I waited for a second, my growing sense of confusion met only by silence. It sounded as if the phone line had gone dead, and then I heard the unmistakable sound of a beer bottle hitting against a wood table. My dad was drinking. And for once in his life, he actually had a good reason. My best friend, Jordan, just sixty-six days after officially becoming a teenager, was dead.

AT A MOMENT like this, everything you think you know about the world, you realize you don't know. You want it to be a joke. You want them to be wrong. You want it to be a dream. And it's none of those things. It's real. And it hurts worse than any other kind of hurt you've ever felt. Jordan, in all his innocence and hilarity and joy and wonder, was dead. And I was still here.

· · ·

JORDAN'S FUNERAL WAS a disaster.

I couldn't believe that my best friend was gone. My memories of him were still so fresh. If I closed my eyes just for a second, I could see him. I could see his hair, the way it never had any particular direction or shape. I could see his smile, both the one he would resort to in moments of timidness and the one that would sneak out in times of joy. I could hear his voice in all its different decibels, and picture the way his eyebrows would dance upward when he told you a story he wanted you to take seriously. I could see all these things, and yet he was gone. It made me so angry. A sense of rage and bubbling betrayal was beating in my chest, screaming to be expressed. As everyone sat there, inside a Catholic church with the sun beating in through the stained glass windows, it was as if the loudest sound in the world was silence. A kid's funeral is not much of a party. I didn't cry at all. I cried before and I cried after, but not there. I wanted to be tough, and I thought that's what tough was. But I missed my friend. I missed him a lot. The hurt I felt was horrible and heavy, like a weight lodged in the center of my chest; impossible to move or make sense of.

I went outside the night after Jordan's funeral and looked up toward the sky. I didn't know whether or not I believed in an afterlife. This whole business of death seemed like some sort of unsolved science experiment. Where do we go? Where did Jordan go? How can someone be here one day and be so vibrant, so real, such a human being—and then be gone the next? It was a soul-crushing question to wrestle with; I guess it still is. I decided to sit down on the grass outside my house and pretend that I could still talk with him; that despite what had happened and why, he could hear my words clear as day. I opened my mouth, but nothing came out. It was as though tragedy had taken everything from me, even my voice. I went back inside and decided to write him a letter.

Dear Jordan,

I guess I know now that the time passes through me and not me through it. There is a moment almost every single day when some sort of remembrance of you shows up and smacks me in the face for attention. Maybe it's a song or a movie or a monkey tree that I see in a park. But it doesn't matter that I'm seeing it in a park because I first saw it in your front yard and that's the only place I will ever be able to remember it. All these things do nothing other than put holes in who I am, and watch me leak out of myself. In your absence I've found myself haunted and hollowed. To think of our times that were shared yesterday and know there will never be a tomorrow is enough to shatter whatever is remaining of my spirit; once innocent before imparted with so much tragedy. I feel these things in my heart—and it aches—but I have a hard time putting them on my tongue. I miss my best friend. I don't want my words to end up as an invitation to tragedy or—even worse—a pedestal for pity. I just want to feel these things because they are the things that I feel. Your companionship was true and it was given without considering whether or not I was worthy of it. Now, with you gone, I wonder if the world was worthy of you.

Your stay was not long enough. Your grace immeasurable. Your truth somewhere embedded into the fabric of my life. I'm honored to say I was changed by your life and horrified to say I have been changed by your death. But even in all this despair, there is still something that can't be dirtied by the cruelty of an early death. And that is you made more of your time than most do. If there's one thing your death taught me, it's just how well you lived. You are a north star for us all, an example for many and a friend of mine. Wherever it is exactly that you are, I know you're making it better just by being there. That's how it always was. And while the leaves fall and the skies look sad and the wind bites harder and some things change, I know that never will.

I COULDN'T BELIEVE that in twenty or so days I was going to have my birthday. I was going to celebrate another year of my life, another year of my existence, while my best friend was never going to get to do the same. Here I was, becoming a teenager, getting ready for high school, and I had no one to go through it with. My best friend was gone, and I didn't have the first clue as to what to do.

I was about to become a teenager, and it felt like my whole life was starting to fall apart.

NOTE TO SELF

Life is beautiful. Death is brutal. And nothing can ever take away true friendship—not even tragedy.

4

High School, Hormones, and Hard-Ons

NO ONE REALLY takes you seriously when you're a teenager, and it's the most awkward of ages. It's a transitional time laced with torturous self-loathing and pimples fighting for prime bodily real estate. It's a sort of in-between time, when your body is betraying you and everyone thinks you should be more mature than you actually are. It's so much easier to be a child than a teenager. When you're a child, you can do almost anything under the license of not knowing better. Like when I was four or five, and my mum was talking to someone on the phone and I was having a bath, and I had to poop. Unwilling to make the costly sacrifice of warmth for personal hygiene, I unburdened myself in the water and just waited to "see what would happen." Not much did, other than that the room started to change odors and my mom came in with a pasta strainer to purify the waters, if you will. When you're a child, sympathy is given to you practically by the truckload. It's as though the world thinks it's kind of cute how much help you need and how disabling simple activities are.

"Oh, look, he can't feed himself!"

"Oh, look, he can't bathe himself!"

Everyone expects you to somehow have things figured out once you're a teenager, as if you've quietly, in the closet of your childhood, been hoarding an abundance of valuable life lessons. The thing about being a teenager is this: you're basically an emotional toddler who thinks he's an adult. You're trapped inside this body that's practically self-combusting, and yet people start talking to you like you're ready to buy a house and grow a garden. It's a very strange experience to go through, all while living inside a science experiment of a body. Hormones and hasty judgment intersect like two drunk drivers running a red light. The teenage years are basically one never-ending internal tug-of-war between your body and your brain. Your body is telling you to have sex with anything that moves and talk to girls, and your brain is telling you to be realistic and accept that you've got the same odds of sexual success as you do of hitting the jackpot at seven slot machines simultaneously in Vegas. Your brain is ready to grow up, but your body is still trying to put hair in places. It's all one big wrestling match.

Body: Go talk to that girl!

Brain: Your balls are the size of watermelon seeds!
And so on.

But there are some good things that happen when you become a teenager. All of a sudden, you have much more freedom and you can go to movies by yourself or leave the house for hours at a time to be with your friends. While I've never been released from prison after serving most of a life sentence for a crime I didn't commit, I have to imagine this is not unlike that experience. So you have independence, and yet your torso is still just trying to fill out a T-shirt and your voice is switching decibels like a bad indie rock concert. The worst part is you can't really relate to anyone other than your peers about it. And even that is a struggle sometimes. People change and grow at different paces. My friend Justin had a mustache in grade nine. A serious, I-buy-porn type of 'stache. I didn't necessarily want a mustache—or to look like someone who would purchase pornography—but still, it made me a bit jealous that he could grow one and I couldn't. I barely had hair in my armpits, and here he was walking around like he had a mortgage. Then there was my friend Nick, who had the chest of a small gorilla by the time we were fifteen or so. My body was almost built inward, as if my pectorals were somehow folding in on one another, and Nick was built like a professional football player. Later he became a professional baseball player, and in my own head it's still because of his prepubescent muscle development.

Almost all of these things feel very unfair. That's mostly what being a teenager is all about: growing through the unfair, awkward awfulness of life and pretending that it's fun. That's essentially what growing up is. It's a messy, sticky, unforgettably bad business mixed with euphoric, druglike states of happiness. And there's absolutely no one there to help you really. I think being a teenager is a lot like getting caught masturbating by your mother: once it's happened, you don't want to mention it, you just want to move on.

So, if you're like me, no one talks to you about what it's like to grow up. It just sort of happens. And you just sort of try to put the pieces where you may. And everything ends up a bit of a blur with a strong overlay of body odor.

MY BIRTHDAY IS in August. September always seems to roll around so fast once it's August. The year I was headed to high school, ready to find my way to the bottom of the social totem pole, it felt like I had my birthday, went to sleep, woke up, and summer was over. Suddenly, the demands of life and showing up to school were all too real.

I really didn't want to go to school that year. I mean, probably only a very small selection of kids want to go to school ever. But I really didn't want to go to high school. It would have been one thing to go back to my old school and bask in the familiar faces and small classes and busted-up water fountains. But this wasn't Willows. This was high school. And high school was something I was supposed to do with Jordan. We had signed up to share that locker. We were supposed to do this together, and now I was alone. I told my mum how I felt, and she was very understanding. Looking back, I realize that she was in a pretty tough position as a parent. That's what happens when people die too soon; no one knows what to do.

So September 4 rolled around and the bus pulled up in front of my house and I got on it. I was wearing a blue and white striped polo tee with an ink stain from a ballpoint pen. Sitting in the back of the bus with my headphones so deep in my ears I thought they might be permanently lodged there, I let myself imagine for a few moments that Jordan was going to be there. As far as thoughts go, it was a beautiful one. I bathed in it, wondering if maybe I would get off the bus and show up at our locker and he would just be there. Standing there in his trademark jacket, smiling, ready to rip into me for believing he was really dead. I could hear his voice dance inside my head, "You *really* believed I was dead?! Fuck you, man." The thought of it put a smile on my face.

Fifteen minutes later, the bus pulled up to school and I shuffled off it, lost in a sea of students and scared absolutely shitless. I followed the herd through the front doors and to the main office, where I got my information for my locker and a handful of judgmental stares from seniors. I

walked quickly and quietly, doing my best not to be noticed, hoping that if I hurried, I could blend right into the
walls and become invisible.

Oak Bay High consisted of two buildings; each was
approximately ten times as big as my last school, and the
hallways were so crowded it looked like a popular night-
club, not a place of education. My locker was tucked far
away, down a dusty hallway that—unlike the others—was
completely vacant, with two skylights in the ceiling and
FAT CHICKS LOVE FAT DICKS! carved into a wall. I stood in
front of my locker and nervously fiddled with the padlock
to open it, less afraid of what I would see when I opened
the small, dented door and much more afraid of what I
wouldn't see: Jordan. I opened the locker. It was completely empty, just like me. Jordan wasn't coming. This
was it. This was life now. I had this whole locker to use
and this whole life to live, and I was going to have to do all
of it without my best friend.

I MADE IT through all of thirty-six hours of high school
before I ended up in the school office. Every kid who gets
called down to the office feels a bit like a criminal facing
an interrogation; you start trying to figure out what you've
done that could have gotten you into trouble. I gathered
my books from class and got up to head to the office, all
the while making a mental list. All I could come up with

was that I had littered, throwing a chocolate milk jug on the field because I couldn't find a garbage can . . . and that I had stolen a book from my sister. I assumed I was probably safe on the literary theft, but the littering had me worried. I wondered if maybe in high school they had cameras all around, like in that book *1984,* and had seen it all happen. I was very nervous about the whole thing, but also strangely thankful for my sadness to be temporarily sidetracked to situational anxiety. It was a welcome relief.

I walked down to the office and introduced myself to the sixty-something-year-old lady behind the desk. She was wearing one of those headsets with a microphone, and it looked like she had no fewer than two thousand Post-it notes stuck to her desk, an artistic display of disorganization.

"Hi. I was told to come down here?"

"Who are you?" she snapped, without making eye contact or using a tone that could be described as either conversational or kind.

"Kevin."

"Do you have a last name, Kevin?"

"Yes. Breel."

"Oh! Kevin BREEL!" she squealed as if we were long-lost friends. "Yes. Here you go."

She handed me an envelope. I took it and opened it up. Made uneasy by her sudden shift from office dictator to amicable ally, I was almost scared to look at what she had handed me. Inside was a small, handwritten note saying that I needed to go down to the auditorium that afternoon. The note was unsigned, unmarked, and completely unnerving. To my knowledge, and up until that moment to my relief, no one here knew I existed. Far too scared to ask who had sent it, I scurried out of the office. High school was off to a seriously weird beginning.

THE AUDITORIUM IN Oak Bay High School was a poor excuse for a theater. The small red seats offered the spinal support of a unicycle, and the stage was chipped and decayed from years of crappy improv classes, dance recitals, and general neglect. I found my way in through the back door and was both relieved and surprised to see that I was late. While the room was dimly lit, I could see that more than half the seats were unoccupied and mostly everyone sat alone, fidgeting, looking at the floor, reeking of nerves and neuroticism. Onstage, a short man with what was either a buzz cut or early signs of baldness, muscular arms, and a thick Australian accent was busy pacing around and speaking. His name was Allen York, and apparently he was the full-time guidance counselor. I found a vacant seat somewhere near the back, using my backpack as a pillow and the darkness as an opportunity for anonymity in case I decided to give in to my desire to take a nap. I was very tired and still didn't know why I had been asked to come to this; more than anything, I wanted to just go home.

The nice thing I'd already noticed about high school was that no one kept track of you. You could basically just leave at any given time, or at least that's what I thought then. The bus stop was right in front of the school, and I could get on the bus and go home when I wanted. You can't do that in middle school. Your teacher will call your mum and your mum will call you and you will end up apologizing often without knowing what you need forgiveness for. I liked that high school seemed to come with an absence of accountability. One of my teachers didn't even do attendance. The whole thing was a paradise for people like me who wanted to gently fall through the cracks of the system, both unnoticed and unbothered.

Allen York kept talking from the stage, and I kept trying not to listen. The guy was persistent though, I'll certainly give him that. He wasn't preachy or loud like most teachers when they take hold of a microphone; in fact, he was quite the opposite. His words were gentle and his face was weathered from both age and what I guessed to be wisdom. He moved frequently and made intense eye contact with the audience, as if his whole world depended on every kid paying attention. At one point, he started talking about some seriously heavy stuff. He said none of us in life can move forward if we still have pain in our heart. He got really passionate about this and said it was okay to have pain and to have problems. "You can be hurt. We all get hurt. But not all of us get help."

He encouraged everyone who was struggling to come

find him and talk to him. For a split second, I wondered
why I had been asked to come here. Looking around, I
saw that the less-than-half-full room was home to some
unique characters, each kid looking like a bad stereotype.
There was a skateboarder dressed in all black with song
lyrics hand-drawn in Wite-Out on his T-shirt and enough
holes in his jeans that you could—willingly or unwill-
ingly—make out half of his groin. There was a goth girl,
who was wearing at least two inches of what was either
eye shadow or Crayon and had six piercings in her face
alone. There were smokers and gangsters and a girl wearing a black beanie and boots with spikes on the side. I
wondered if this was a meeting of the fuckups. Before I
could let myself feel angry for being guilty by association,
Allen York's voice grabbed my attention again. He talked
more about the importance of "asking for help" and made
sure we knew we were "always welcome" in his office.

I tended to want to strangle adults who put on the "I'm
just here to help you children" mask, but something about
Allen was different. He genuinely did seem like he cared
and wanted to help. Just as the smallest part of me was beginning to open up to him, the bell blasted twice and the
lights got bright again and the speech was over. Kids filed
out to their next class—or to a gang meeting, depending
on whose schedule you were following—and I decided to
walk out the front doors and head home. Even with all the
awful stuff that was happening—missing Jordan, starting

at a new school, still being skinny—it was nice to be able to do that. I thought about how Jordan would have loved it. I felt the tears start to pool up, and like a well-trained dog scaring off an intruder, I chased the thought right out of my mind.

I got home, had a glass of milk, laid on the couch, tried to watch TV, got bored, drank more milk, and then decided I needed to do something. The weather in Victoria in September is not unlike the weather in Victoria in July, and so I figured I might as well go outside and enjoy the last of it. I put on a pair of shorts and a T-shirt, grabbed a basketball from my bedroom, and went down to Maynard Park. I shot around for ten minutes or so. I prefer to play basketball when it's not so hot. I don't like my own shadow on the court. I know that's a weird thing to have an aversion to, but it's true. If I can see my shadow on the court, it means the sun is too strong and it's too hot for me. And I could see my shadow today. So after ten minutes I decided to call it quits and head back home. Right as I walked off the court, though, out of the corner of my eye, I saw someone walking two giant, intimidating-looking dogs. The kind of dogs who looked like they should either be searching you for drugs or protecting someone else's drugs. Even though I was at a healthy distance, they looked like they could dismantle me in half a minute if they needed to and might even find enjoyment in the experience. One of my worst fears in life has always been being attacked by a dog.

I can picture myself on the ground, rolling around with my arms covering my person, flailing about screaming "NOT THE BALLS! NOT THE BALLS!" Distracted by my own daydream, what I didn't notice right away was who was walking them. It was the man from stage earlier, Allen York. I couldn't believe it. Here I was skipping school, and here he was skipping work. Ironic. I was about to just keep on walking, but there was something about the situation that made me brave it out and go up to him. While I waited for my brain to shoot down the idea, it didn't.

"Hey, are you Allen York?"

"Yes, I am. Who might you be?" I was almost expecting him to say "chap" at the end of that. His Aussie accent was even thicker up close, hugging every single syllable.

"I'm Kevin Breel."

"Kevin Breel! Oh, wow. What a small world. I have you on the top of my list for tomorrow."

"Your list?"

"Yes. I . . ." His voice started to trail off, as if he was thinking about more things than he could possibly manage to say. He paused, swallowed, and started over. "You were close with Jordan McGregor, yes?"

"Yeah. How do you know that?"

"Because we spent the summer identifying which kids were his friends that are at our school now. Your name came up the most. You guys must have been close."

"Yeah. Yeah, we were." Talking about Jordan in the past tense was a hard adjustment for me to make. It made me feel gross, as if the words rotted my soul before they could come out of my mouth.

"Well, the school has a strict rule about making sure students who lost someone they were close to get proper grief counseling. So you're on the top of my list tomorrow. I'll buzz your classroom and you can come to my office and we'll talk."

"Um . . . I think it'll be fine. I mean . . ."

"Just come tomorrow. Come down and talk. Okay?"

"Sure." When the word came out of my mouth, I couldn't believe it. It came out reluctantly and without the slightest inclination toward real excitement, but it came out nonetheless. The mere action of agreeing had left me both ashamed and astonished.

THE FIRST HOUR I spent with Mr. York was friendly and pleasant. He was interested in me—not in the false, pretend way that most adults are but in a real way. We talked easily. I even laughed a few times. Plus, I got to skip class. That part seemed irrefutably awesome. I left thinking that maybe this whole counseling thing wasn't so bad after all.

After that, we were supposed to sit down once a week in his office overlooking the parking lot and the giant willow tree that hid almost every car from view. His office was small and cramped and looked a bit like someone had put a thousand tiny pieces of paper on his desk and then turned on a fan full blast. It was a war zone of stationery and sticky notes.

"How's class? How's home? How's Kevin?" he was fond of asking. His concern for me was so geniune and piercing that it made me uncomfortable. I preferred to ignore such care. More than anything, though, I preferred to ignore my own feelings; and so I would avoid talking about myself whenever possible. Allen would always keep pushing, neither too forcefully nor too gently. Just enough to show that he cared and was there to catch me, if I ever decided to fall out of my hardened shell of emotional control and cautious honesty, something I mistook for safety. As much as his questions made me nervous, his concern felt reassuring. When Jordan died, it felt like everything I knew had been taken away from me. Not only did I lose my best friend, but it felt like I lost my second family, too. Jim and Jordan had been a home away from home. I lived with girls, and these were two guys who had understood me. They got me. And now all that was gone. I felt alone and invisible. If nothing else, Mr. York made me feel seen again.

Halfway through that school year, I started to sink into intense despair. The truth was, my heart was aching without Jordan. I had spent so much time keeping my feet moving forward, I hadn't ever really let the weight of his death sink in. Sometime during the winter the bleakness started to bleed into all corners of my life, like red paint on a white canvas. I was a destructive combination of angry and sad. Mr. York kept asking me to come to see him, and I kept skipping the sessions. When I felt like the world was out to get me, the last place I wanted to be was in his tiny, cramped office tucking my knees into my chest and handing my heart over to whoever wanted to take a look. So I ditched school more and more often, skipped out on meeting with Mr. York, and hid in my little hole of a room.

Things got worse. As much as I'd initially thought that in high school no one knew what you were up to—or cared to find out—it was becoming clear that that wasn't true. I was one of Allen's responsibilities now. Because of this, the school was calling home and leaving messages for my mum. So, in an effort to outsmart the system, I used to come home and wait for the school's automated voice mail to call our house to let my mum know I had skipped school. I would let it ring and then delete the message and erase the caller ID from the phone log. It worked perfectly. I had found the cracks in the system, and I was content to let myself fall through them.

Unfortunately, or fortunately, Mr. York didn't share the sentiment. He had dedicated his life to helping kids, and he wasn't about to change that for me. Always a few steps ahead of me, he started calling the house, too. So now I was deleting two callers and two messages a day. It felt like a part-time job. Plus, the pay was shit. But it worked for a while. And then one afternoon, while the cold came and parked itself inside my house, I listened to a voice mail Mr. York had left on my home phone.

"Hi, this is Allen York. This message is for Kevin. You missed our session today. But that's not why I'm calling. I'm calling because I haven't seen your face for a while and I hope you're doing okay. I know you haven't been coming to class. That's okay. But I need you to let me know how you're doing. You have to let me know how you're doing. So call me back or I will come over to your house. You need to let me know that you're okay. By the end of the day. Okay? Thanks."

That message killed me. Every part of me that felt unworthy and unwanted was washed with his concern and, as sappy as it might sound, his love in that moment. It was a strange but sensational change from the frequent feeling of being damaged and defective. I know now that it was the most special gift delivered at the most important moment. But then I just thought I should call him back. I did, and we talked on the phone for about thirty minutes. I promised to come see him in his office the next week and talk. He encouraged me, the way he always did, and I hung up the phone with a strange feeling inside my chest: hope.

NOW THAT I was back on the counseling wagon, things started to improve again. Mr. York started filling me up with pep talks every few days, telling me that things would get better and challenging me to make them that way. "You don't get 'over' this stuff, Kevin. You get *through* it," he would remind me, his Australian accent hanging off every syllable, making his words sound smarter somehow. He really was an incredible man, an example of both strength and softness. He was a gentle guide and a booming voice of truth. And I was far from being an easy kid to work with. Often I would get enraged with him, challenging his perspective on everything important and cursing him out for his "bullshit cashmere sweaters." I had nothing but gratitude inside for him, really. It's just that my way of showing it was often coated in rage.

He would never take any of my words personally, though I'm not sure how. And I, of course, managed to find a way to take his indifference and turn it into outrage. One afternoon, as tears fell out of my eyes and words I didn't mean made their way out of my mouth, I told him that I thought he should take his degrees and shove them up his ass. Or something similarly poetic.

"You don't know anything! You went to school and read a book! I'M LIVING THIS! Don't you understand that? THIS IS MY LIFE. I have to wake up every morning and be me. And you don't. Don't you get that?" I shouted at him, sounding far less convincing than I had imagined I would.

Mr. York paused and smiled and swiveled in his chair,

then pulled the blinds down. I thought he was about to roll up his sleeves and sock me in the mouth. I wouldn't have blamed him. Instead, he leaned forward in his chair, resting his elbows on his knees, and looked me square in the eyes, making sure I wasn't going to miss a single word he said, the same way he had been the first day I saw him back in that auditorium.

"Kevin. You know something? I grew up in Australia. I played rugby. I was this rumble, tumble, tough kid. A lot tougher than you, actually. I thought I had life figured out, you know?" He spoke slowly, letting my breathing return to normal and my tears slow from a waterfall to a gentle drip.

"I didn't have anything figured out though. I ran away from home and I started doing drugs. Not the light drugs either, the hard stuff, the stuff you need needles for." He kept that brilliant eye contact, as if he wanted to watch my pupils get larger in pure shock at what was coming out of the mouth of this person who to me seemed like the poster child of boring, conservative life choices.

"You wanna see something? I'll show you something." He now peeled off the purple cashmere sweater that was tightly hugging his massive shoulders. My gray-haired, sixty-year-old counselor was apparently taking his shirt off. This certainly wasn't how they portrayed therapy in the movies. He swiveled his chair around so that his back was facing me.

"You see that?" he asked.

I couldn't believe what I was seeing. Scars, running all along his back, some of them six inches long. You could even see where the stitches used to be: long, crisscrossed patterns that were ugly and harsh.

"Yes, I do," I replied meekly, nodding.

"You know what that's from? That's from the knife of a drug dealer. I got into an argument with him over ten bucks of crank, and he robbed me. Right in the back of an alley. Stabbed me in the back and left me to die. I was living on the streets, and these were the kind of people who I dealt with every day. I didn't go get those degrees on my wall because I'm such a shiny example of perfection, Kevin. I got them because I'm the opposite. I'm imperfect. Just like you. Just like everyone around you. Just like the entire world.

"I know what it's like to be fucked up. And that's why I want to help you. The way I see it, you have two choices. The first? You keep doing what you're doing. You keep showing up to school. You keep coming to talk to me. You keep doing the work and telling me what's in your heart, and I will keep doing my best to help you. I will do anything I can to help you. The second? You don't show up anymore. You keep skipping school. You stay at home. You sink deeper and deeper into your dark little world, and you live there. That's fine. I'll just come drive my truck to your house, knock on your door, and drag you out of your room. I might be old, but I'm still a lot fucking stronger than you are. Anyway, our time's up for today."

And with that, he pulled his purple cashmere sweater back over his body, reopened the blinds, and led me out of his office.

I was confused, amazed, and, for the first time in my life, confident that I had a man in my corner who cared about me . . . maybe even more than I was willing to care about myself.

I WISH THAT the next part of this story was about how I showed up to counseling every day and got better. I wish it was all about how I let Allen York speak truth into my life, and how he changed me for good. How I danced off into the sunset with a brimming optimism. Instead, I did what any kid who has been kicked, rejected, hurt, and abandoned does: I pushed Mr. York away. The sessions were just getting too tough, and his unyielding concern was too much to carry. A few weeks after he gave me his shirtless keynote speech, he started asking me to write out what I was feeling and bring it in. He said there are things that sometimes we don't even know are in us until we let them out. I thought that sounded absolutely silly and like something that should be printed on a shitty coffee mug. But my sister found out about this—through the fault of my big, fat, unfilterable mouth—and bought me a brown leather journal to write in. She wasn't home much, and she had a penchant for pissing me off when she was, but deep down she was the most wonderful young woman I knew, with a heart bigger than our house.

I took the journal and tried to write things for about a week. At the end of seven days, I had four pages, mostly all crossed out, and a drawing of a mountain; one that looked more like something a five-year-old who had put a pencil in his mouth had scribbled than a protruding force of nature. I was pissed off and told Mr. York this. He said something about patience or persistence. I heard "stop being a lazy piece of shit." Whatever the advice, it worked.

He had won me over. I got on the bus, went back home, and started writing.

A FEW DAYS later I showed up at his office and handed him one slightly crumpled, messy piece of paper, which held the blueprint to my first ever poem. I put it on his desk and left his office.

It read:

I'm in the middle of a road
Looking for a destination
But it does not yet exist
Or maybe
I'm just looking in the wrong direction entirely

I hear people say they love me
I hope they don't lie to me
Because it's lonely over here
And I need to feel whole
So please, just look at me and smile
And don't ask what's in my soul
Because it's filled with too many holes
This all looked so much better when I was peeking
    through the window
I don't like being on the inside of all this glass
But I was the one
Who walked into the room
But
I hope it all gets dark soon
I care no longer for the lights
I wish no more for shine
I feel better all alone in the dark
And that's not so new
This tortured, dark and blackened heart
Really, it's who I've been from the start

MR. YORK READ it and instantly called my mum. He brought the three of us together for a meeting, something which had never happened before, and I spent the majority of the time looking at the floor. Eventually he asked me to leave the room so he could speak to my mum privately. She told me later that he thought I was dangerously depressed, even suicidal. He asked her if she thought I would rather be with Jordan.

She cried and nodded her head yes.

Mr. York brought me back in and told me he wanted me to start seeing him three times a week, that we needed to double down on our efforts, work three times as hard, and really fix this thing while we still could.

Instead, I filled out the paperwork to switch schools the next day.

NOTE TO SELF

Good advice is hard to find and even harder to accept. Accept it anyway. One day, you'll wake up and wish you had done it sooner.

5

Hurry Up, Get Your Heart Crushed

AFTER I SWITCHED schools yet another time, it started to dawn on me that some of what Allen had said was true: I was definitely lonely. In comparison to my relationship with Jordan, all my other friendships felt almost fake, like I was forcing something that I wanted to be there but wasn't really. Where I could once count on Jordan's unique, empathetic companionship, I now felt judged, scrutinized, and misunderstood. People didn't get me, my stories, my insecurities, or my jokes. It seemed like other people were nothing more than a mirror to remind me what a great friend I had lost, and I hated them for it. I knew this was deeply unfair—harsh, even—but I couldn't be bothered to change. Jordan had become the measuring stick for all my relationships, and no one could come close to matching what he had meant to me. My reaction to this was part self-defense and part self-sabotage; I pushed everyone who had once been close to the edges of my life.

More and more, I spent my time alone. I didn't let people into my stuff, and I even did a pretty good job disguising the fact that I had any stuff. But as much as I had resisted, resented, and rejected so much of Allen's advice, I had to admit that it was starting to make sense. I was desperately alone and slowly being suffocated by my own solitude. My heart had been hurt by losing Jordan, and each day that I spent alone, the walls around the isolation seemed to harden a little bit more. My way of coping was to run away from everything that hurt, even if what I was running toward was far worse than what I was leaving behind. It was the only way I knew how to deal with my problems. Jordan had left me, so I was going to leave everyone and everything else that made me feel broken. I thought in some way I could fix myself by wrecking everything else.

So I went off to a new high school. My mum supported my decision to go, and I was thankful for it. While she was an advocate for the conversations Mr. York and I were having, she also understood that the scenery at Oak Bay was suffocating. Each day, being around a group of kids who reminded me of Jordan—or rather, the lack thereof—I felt like a pinball, bouncing from one painful memory to the next.

As far as high schools go, Lambrick Park could only

be described as uncomfortable. The hallways were tight and narrow and the gym was dusty and old and there were twelve guys for every girl. Seriously. The testosterone was so palpable you could almost taste it. And it tasted terrible: like a mixture of fear and puberty.

Despite the imbalanced numbers and the relative newness of my school, I was determined to find someone to care about. Reluctantly, I had begun to realize that the words Mr. York had shared with me were true: I needed other people in my life. And now, full of hormones and hell-bent on having sex, I wanted to find love. It was a bold, brash hope for someone who felt as socially handicapped as I did.

IF I WAS certain of one thing, it was this: girls are confusing. Deeply, horribly confusing. I had adopted the rather astute belief that all women shot straight out of the womb with a manual in their hands entitled "How to Fuck with Men: A Practical Guide." I mean, most guys—especially the ones trapped in the teenage years—are already confused enough as it is, so it's hardly a difficult job. But girls do it the best, as though it is genetically preconditioned.

At any given point during high school, I was being misled, misdirected, misguided, and generally mystified by no fewer than thirty-three girls at a time. Of course, no more than five of these girls would actually "know about my existence," but I didn't let such small obstacles hold me back from the idea that I was closely pursuing all of them. As a rule of thumb, girls will frustrate you to the exact level you adore them. More bluntly: anyone who you put on a pedestal is going to use that pedestal to get a better opening position from which to jump on and crush your heart. Okay, maybe it's not that bad. But it's probably close. High school girls know this; they practically take pride in it. While you could argue that these sorts of mind games are generated from hormones, I think it's much more than that. It's primal, like a rite of passage of some kind. They are learning their power, pushing the limits progressively further. Often, I wondered if they gathered together to have makeshift meetings, each going around the room sharing a story from the week. "So then I told him, 'You can only date me if you agree to keep pursuing me for another six months, with no sexual contact or social acknowledgment of any kind and . . .'" If there's a teenage girl somewhere in the world who won't make you feel like crap for having a crush on her, I certainly never met her. Even if she likes you, too, she'll find a way.

I'd like to make it very clear that I'm not saying women are mean. I don't think women are mean at all. In fact, quite the contrary. Most women are kind and compassionate and overflowing with empathy. But we're not talking about women here. We're talking about a whole separate breed of the female species. We're talking about young, teenage girls; and young, teenage girls are about as similar to women as gasoline is to water. Teenage girls have a compass pointing to your deepest insecurities and are not afraid to tell everyone else exactly where they are, too.

BUT BOYS CAN be equally cruel to girls; it's just that if they're like me, it's often unknowingly. I went to elementary school with this girl named Simone. She was really tall—taller than me, actually, which evoked an odd combination of embarrassment and awe—and slim and actually quite pretty for being twelve and in the middle of having every single part of her body change. She had dark brown hair and olive skin and got dropped off at school in a car with no roof. I had never seen a convertible before and so therefore jumped to the conclusion that her life outside of school was probably very closely aligned with that of an action movie. Simone had this bubbly personality that pretty much overflowed her; she was always half laughing when she talked or smiled. She told everyone she was going to be a model, and shockingly, she actually became a model. More shockingly, she had the audacity to have a crush on me and be rather kind about the whole thing. I found out that Simone liked me from her friend Olivia, who was also quite pretty; but she had a crush on my friend Aden, who, much to his own credit, seemed more interested in winning the approval of a fly than of a woman. So Olivia told me Simone liked me, and I did what I thought was romance: pretending I didn't care at all, while actually caring a lot.

It took me the better part of a week to finish fully processing the idea that someone of the opposite gender had a feeling other than that of absolute repulsion toward me. Every day after that, I thought of ways to hang out with Simone. Obviously, I really didn't need to think of reasons to hang out with a girl who already liked me. But I didn't know this then; rational thought rarely finds a home in a young boy's brain.

Simone and I would talk in the back of Mr. Walker's class, and I always remember having a feeling in my stomach similar to when a roller coaster drops down and you feel like you're either going to soil your pants or vomit on the person in front of you. One day I settled on asking her to play basketball with me because I'm a boy and I'm dumb. I didn't know that exactly zero girls on planet Earth want to throw a dirty ball at a piece of circular metal to bond with a boy they like. Somehow, despite this, she agreed, and I felt excited for about a second and then completely terrified for the rest of the day. The whole afternoon, with the waiting mixture of anticipation and anxiety, it felt like I had jumped into a well of fear with no foreseeable way out other than crying out, "I TOLD YOU GUYS I COULDN'T DO THIS SHIT!"

Finally, right as my arteries were about to explode, the

bell rang and the day was over and Simone and I ended up playing basketball. I missed almost every shot and at least three chances to kiss her. After about an hour, her mom came and picked her up. I watched from the court as she drove off with Simone and my self-esteem. I told all of this, confessional style, to my friends Chris and Brandon, and they told me I'd done the right thing. Chris specifically said Simone was gross and told me—to quote—"not to touch her beard."

It's worth stating that Chris also had a massive crush on Simone. I, however, did not know this. The reason I did not know this was because Chris was constantly trying to humiliate Simone. He said she had facial hair and an Adam's apple. I never understood this, as none of us guys were even capable of growing a beard and/or producing a visible display of an Adam's apple, every teenage guy's longed-for badge of masculinity. The way I saw it was that even if Simone did have a beard, it would be a bit more humiliating for all of us than it would be for her, at least in my books. But Chris just kept on saying it.

"Heyyyyyy, Simoneeeee! Your beard is growinnnnn'!"

Eventually it stuck with some people. I guess if you repeat stuff long enough, people think you had a reason to say it in the first place. What I didn't grasp at the time was that a teenage boy who professes his disdain for a girl is actually really just confessing his unfiltered love for her. It's as though in every guy's mind, the fastest path to getting a girl is to make her feel like shit, as if her tears will somehow start to act as a natural love lubricant.

Not knowing Chris was secretly in love with the girl I was in love with, I allowed his comments to get into my head, and I started to get worried that I shouldn't like Simone. After all, it seemed like popular opinion was that she was some sort of circus freak, and I didn't want to be left on the sidelines, holding my heart in one hand and social humiliation in the other. So I stopped talking to Simone and essentially let myself be persuaded out of pursuing a girl by a guy who also wanted to pursue her. It was a perfect love triangle, a devastating combination of embarrassment, dishonesty, and raging hormones.

But back to high school.

IT WAS MY freshman year and I was convinced I had it all figured out. I was going to wear a tuxedo and take a girl to the prom. We would dance and open a bottle of champagne—not to drink but just to see the cork fly off—and I would lose my virginity in a field, which despite its seemingly unforgiving nature would be both comfortable and private. The moon would shine above us, and we would whisper to each other about how we would be together forever and how every moment would be as wonderful as this one. I may have been young, but my mental grasp on what a real relationship looked like was genius.

It was around the time I entered into the unfamiliar waters of my new high school that I met Vanessa. She was short with tanned skin and long wavy hair and a penchant for pulling me along on emotional roller coasters. In hindsight, I see that her life lacked a lot of stability, and she probably enjoyed knowing one thing was stable: that she could grab, stomp on, and spit on my heart without much argument from me. So that's probably why everything went the way it did. Sadly, you don't know these sorts of things when you're fourteen. And even if you did, it wouldn't do much to tame the circus already under way in your pants. So you would probably just get hurt all the same. Vanessa taught me that all girls were complicated and came with a set of rules.

Vanessa's biggest rule was that she would never start a conversation with you. I really wish I was making this stuff up because it would save me a lot of the shame. She would blatantly tell you to your face—unflinchingly and without any trace of feeling—that she would not initiate a conversation with you. The way she said it made it sound normal, which is quite an accomplishment in itself. Even if she liked you, she wouldn't start talking to you. Especially if she liked you, actually. And of course, by talking, I really mean texting. No one talks anymore. Talking is for war veterans and lawyers and the elderly. This was high school, and in high school, you don't talk to girls, you text them. As the song suggests, the first text is the deepest. Okay, maybe that's not how that song goes. Whatever. What's important is that I—and every other guy waiting in line to experience the wonderful world of Vanessa's bullshit—had to text her first. Of course, to a teenage guy this is frustrating, fascinating, and addictive all at the same time. A guy would be interested in a bag of sand if it could emotionally drag him across the universe the way a girl can.

At any given time, Vanessa had about fourteen guys trying to be her boyfriend. At most, she would typically think two of them were potential candidates but keep the other twelve around as added motivation for the main two to work harder. She was really running a business more than she was a social life. And her business was to get the most committed, caring guy she could and then proceed to mentally devastate that poor individual.

The paradoxical part about all of this was she really wasn't a bad person. She isn't a bad person today, either. She's a good enough person. She just happens to be a good person who does a bad job noticing how she makes other people feel. Part of that you could call selfishness, but the other part of it you would have to call ignorance. She doesn't know she's doing it—not because she doesn't care, but simply because she doesn't take the time to think about it. For her to know she is being mean or hurtful would come with the assumption that she is looking to see how you feel. She isn't. She's simply thinking about how she feels.

That spring she had a big party at her house. The air was warm and thick and I felt alive with possibility. Despite being almost allergic to social situations as large in size as a house party, I decided that I would go, able to forget my fears by hanging on to the hope that Vanessa and I would kiss that night. I was such a ball of sexual tension that I had to wear pants that were a bit too big for me just so that everyone wouldn't notice I was walking around with a boner. I showed up, stinking of cheap cologne and nerves, and within forty-five minutes of arriving, I watched helplessly as she made out with no fewer than four different guys, none of them being me. At one point I walked outside to find a friend and accidentally ran into her making out with a guy on the porch. I turned around right away, in the name of both shame and sexual privacy, and in that same instant, yet *another* guy—this one older, uglier, yet more self-assured—pulled up in his car, and Vanessa, in one smooth motion of boldness and bitchiness, told the guy she just kissed to get her a drink, walked down the stairs, and started making out with the new guy.

If having a chance with a girl is considered "being in the game," I was somewhere near the freeway holding a foam finger, a can of Coca-Cola, and a sign that said I'M CLUELESS. She would wind me up and tear me down, and do it all in a way that made me want to start from square one and win her over. To an observing, rational mind, it's likely hard to see the appeal in continually coming back. But I had put my self-worth into getting a piece of her heart, which pulled me forward each day, and let me take the blows of embarrassment and rejection and turned them into fuel. But this had crossed a line.

While I've never been addicted to heroin, in some ways I imagine that hanging around Vanessa was not unlike that. The largest distinction being: at least if I was addicted to heroin, I would have a legitimate reason to keep on coming back. This, however, made no sense. It was harsh and hurtful—a long one-way street of disappointment, rejection, and confusion. At least if you do drugs, you might get to see something cool. This was pretty much the exact opposite.

As I walked home that night, stunned and ashamed, I was convinced love was not made for me. I wondered whether or not this was because the outside of me was ugly or because the inside was. Perhaps both. I was too scared to actually find out the answer. I had thrown myself into what I thought was intimacy, and now, I simply felt discarded . . . I disgusted myself. Now, as I examined myself closely under the microscope of my deflated masculinity, I saw that it had been ignorance, not bravery, which had brought me to this brutal pursuit of "love."

Time passed. I fell in and out of lust with a few other girls, but after a while, it became hard to say whether I wanted to be in love or was simply in love with the idea of being in love. I know now that to be truly loved, you have to be truly known. To be truly known, you have to be vulnerable. And to be vulnerable, you have to accept your imperfections. You have to accept the parts of your person that stick out: ugly, defiantly disgusting, a mirror for all the many things that you find to be intolerable about your own existence. Without those things, you can't really be loved. You can feel moments of love, but they are fleeting. Temporary. I guess somewhere between hoping for hand jobs and instead receiving heartache, I started to figure this out.

I was scared by the very idea of surrendering my secrets, the ones that had been so well protected by my personality. So well protected that, in truth, I was unsure whether I could ever give them up. Later, I would realize this was not so much an act of self-awareness as it was self-defense. The more I realized love could not be earned, only given, the more it scared the shit out of me. I wanted it all to be easy and effortless. Like a piece of mail, I was hopeful it would come find me, showing up on my front door, ready to be opened up and enjoyed. When it didn't, I reasoned that it was because of who I was, someone beaming a bright light that read "UNLOVABLE."

When you're a guy, waiting for facial hair to grow and measuring your genitals, you don't want to think about things like this. I hated myself for this notion that I needed to be loved. The very idea that it could matter or be meaningful sounds like something your drunk, divorced uncle would talk about when you were a kid. All of this stuff was so hard for me to wrap my head around that it took me forever to figure out the truth.

The truth, though, as clearly as I can see it, is that all of us are made for love. And it's like our horniness is a Trojan horse to bring us into the battlefield of intimacy, and once we're inside, we feel the walls closing in all around us, the lights going off, and the doors locking. It's freaky at first, like you've crossed over an invisible line that you can't come back from. Mainly though it's scary and uncertain because you have to put yourself out there. You have to take risks and let someone into your life. You have to be raw, real, exposed and transparent. I hated this with a venomous passion and protected myself—my heart, my ego, my pride—with every cell in my body.

Slowly though, I began to accept that the idea that I had been sold on—the one which says love is nothing more than an incredible addition to our lives—was a lie. In truth, love is not a missing puzzle piece; it's the foundation from which we build all. It's the fuel we are desperately in need of, male or female, young or old. What I didn't know yet though, the thing that still eluded me until recently, is that love, sex, and intimate relationships are not all synonyms. The infectious feeling of love comes with different labels, in different shapes, in different sizes. I thought then that love was just a bridge to the bedroom, and I found out later it's really a bridge to healing our brokenness.

Maybe this was the root of everything that followed. Maybe all my problems and my pain were tied up in my loneliness. The truth was, I didn't feel loved. Instead, I felt like a defective product, shot off the assembly line of the human factory much too soon, absorbing nothing but scrapes, bruises, and shame ever since.

NOTE TO SELF

Love takes vulnerability. Love takes work.
Girls take all your confidence and crush
it. (Come on, you know you do.)

6

Confused

I CAN'T PINPOINT the exact moment when I first felt that the world was pushing an agenda to "be happy" on me, but I almost can. As a really young kid, I remember watching television when I got home from school. It would usually be three or four in the afternoon, and the television at that time of day is not necessarily designed for the thinking man. I was just becoming old enough to be able to understand that the commercials weren't a part of the show. But all was still a stream of entertainment shooting out of this little box. I didn't quite understand how the box worked. I still don't. And I definitely didn't understand money or marketing or anything like that. So I didn't completely grasp where ads came from or what their purpose was. But I knew that when I was watching a cartoon and then suddenly I was staring at some dude in boots and flannel driving a Dodge Ram, the latter had nothing to do with the former. That much I knew for sure.

There was one ad for McDonald's that always used to play back then during those dulled-out afternoons in front of the television. The commercial had five or six kids sitting outside, and they were having a bad day because their soccer game had been canceled. Maybe it wasn't soccer, but that's how I remember it; whatever it was, they were wearing their fictionalized despair all over their dimpled little faces. The camera panned around and showed them from a wide angle; it was raining and they looked very pissed off and pouty. Just when it seemed like all hope was lost and the world was going to blow up into a million little pieces of prepubescent disappointment, in a plot twist of capitalistic genius, Ronald McDonald showed up on the scene waving his giant hand around and looking all happy. He didn't drive up in a car, but suddenly a car appeared and even though there were eight of them and he was in a sports car, they all fit inside and he took them all to McDonald's and they got free Happy Meals. And as the name would suggest, the kids got their nutritionally handicapped meals while proceeding to get much happier. Everyone started smiling and the camera panned in on the joy on a girl's face, and then a close-up of some grease shining on the fries. Fun music started to play and the commercial ended with the kids jumping in the air dancing, all of them reborn into a place of eternal, unwavering happiness.

It really was a great ad. They probably made millions from it. But this idea of happiness—that we were missing it and needed to find it, force it to the ground, and demand that it be ours—started to grow inside of me. It seemed like all the commercials had the same plot: someone would be unhappy and then he would get something and be happy. I felt like that about naps and graham crackers sometimes, but I never saw any ads on TV for those.

Every day, the outside world tries to works its influence in a little bit more in forming our beliefs about happiness. It's subtle, small stuff mostly. The way when you ask people how they're doing, and they never actually take time to think about the question, they just say, "I'm great, how about you?" Or how all music videos are shot in amazing nightclubs with cool lights and people who are better-looking than you. Everyone looks happy. Everyone around you wants to be happy. It seemed like some days society was screaming at me to be happy. I felt like the only person on earth who wasn't listening.

It's not that I was never happy. I was. I was happy a lot. It's just that as you grow up, the things that make you happy change. But the motivation for wanting to feel happy doesn't really change. It's like the ultimate drug. You forget about everything when you're happy. It's like you get to stop living in your head and start living in your heart or something. So sometimes life, myself, whatever, would all make sense. I would be feeling amazing, and I would think it would be so great to feel this way forever.

And it would all click. But then sometimes it would go away. I would take a look around and see things that sucked everywhere. I would go downtown and see someone living on the street, or someone addicted to drugs, or a cop arresting someone. All of that didn't seem very happy. I don't know when I learned that life was a balance of good and bad, right and wrong. But with every year that passed, I found it harder and harder to accept that I was supposed to just be happy that my life was okay, and not let the fact that millions of other people were suffering in unimaginable ways rain on my parade.

It seemed sometimes like happiness was, at best, a pleasurable distraction from the truth. And the truth, as clearly as I could see it, was that life was hard and hollow, pushing some people toward facing that pain and pulling others toward pretending that everything was perfect.

Could a kid's problems in life really be solved by a cheeseburger? Does a new car really make everyone's existence that much better? It was hard to wrap my head around. But then every time I started to really feel strongly about this stuff, sure enough, something good would happen—a friendly smile, a word of encouragement, a special moment—and I would feel happy all over again and remember that this was indeed the good stuff. Childhood is a constant seesaw of these moments.

When you're really young, the seesaw tends to balance out pretty evenly. Even when bad things happened to me at school or stuff was going on at home or when I was getting bullied, life pretty much always found a way to balance it out to some degree. There were always enough good times to forget about the bad for a bit. But when you become a teenager, the seesaw starts to tip the other way. At least it did for me. It tipped so hard in the other direction that I fell right off, taking bruises on my body and sand in my mouth.

I WAS SIXTEEN years old and I hated myself. I hated my face: the way it was long and angular and how my nose was so pointy, it was almost sharp. I hated that my ears were two different sizes, hated it so much that I would never bring it up to anyone, not even as a joke, because then I would have to wonder every time they looked at me if they were thinking about my ears. And even if they weren't thinking about my ears, I would be, because I hated them. So I hated myself, and the way that I hid it was through what looked like devastating and radical self-acceptance. I made sure everyone else thought I was in love with myself, almost to the point of narcissism, so that they wouldn't think I wasn't normal or something equally awful. I kept my deep self-loathing buried well beneath the layer I let everyone look at. I made sure it stayed that way, as if it was my own personal, wonderful secret that was so good I wouldn't dare spoil it by offering it up to the masses.

I was secretly spiteful about who and what I was and

yet I projected the exact opposite. I was something of a big ball of hypocrisy, waiting to be sliced open and exposed for my own fallacies and fears. Everything about me drove me nuts. The way my voice sounded when I sang along to my favorite songs. How when I looked at myself in the mirror without a shirt on, I could see my three lower ribs poking out, as if to say, "Hey, you're still just a skinny piece of shit!" I hated the way my body occasionally bore dark freckles, similar to the ones trademarked by my father. I hated how my wrists were still as skinny as a child's, and how my thighs were barely thicker than my shoulders. Mostly, I hated how I had to keep on trying to pretend I didn't hate myself.

I had nothing interesting inside of me—not a story, thought, or feeling. The most exciting part about me was my pursuit of deception, every day a new battle in trying to make others believe things about me that I did not believe about myself. It was both disgusting and deeply empty. I was in a well of self-loathing, swimming in personal pity, drowning in pain. My clothes were stupid and I would never invite anyone to my house because, much like my character, it looked much better from the outside than it did on the inside. I was living a life that was both lonely and lackluster, and each day that passed by, I lost more and more of the willpower required to do anything about it.

. . .

THERE ARE A handful of questions you might find yourself with the urge to ask at some point in your life. And sometimes asking these questions will lead somewhere good. Other times the questions will be met with silence.

Some of these questions will be small. Like, why does daylight savings happen? And, why does my dick shrink in swimming pools? But it's the bigger questions—the ones that bounce back and forth in your mind all day, the ones you desperately want to understand—that tend to have the fewest answers.

It was fall of my senior year when I got stuck inside some really bizarre questions. I finally, at least in my own mind, had a leg out the door of my awkwardness. I could see the light at the end of the adolescent tunnel and I felt almost grown up, eager to become an adult. I was fresh, encouraged, and ready to tackle the tough ideas of the universe. Or, more accurately, I thought I was. It started out small: I picked up a few books in a decaying old coffee shop near downtown. The coffee beans smelled like they had been overcooked and the windows were always so steamed up you could see neither in nor out. The same people seemed to rotate in and out of there every single day, an eccentric collection of individuals. But, despite the almost offensive odors and strange social scene, the place always had good books in the back. Most of them were spiritually driven ones, exploring ideas like God or religion or existentialism. I devoured all of them, seemingly unable to digest the information fast enough. I really thought I was becoming a deep thinker. My friend Tony used to say that "sometimes, the problem with going deep is you don't realize you're a few feet away from going off the deep end." I used to wonder what that meant, but that was long before any of this happened.

Those books, ripped, stained, and weathered from use, became an entry point into what was a very odd and roughly carved path for me to begin to walk down. I guess the thing was this: at every turn of my life, I had come face-to-face with pain. My family. School. Friendship. My body. Girls. All of it had blended together into this one blurry picture of pain and rejection and unworthiness. There had been good moments too, some bright moments and some laughs and some love, but there was always a lot of ugly in there. The thing about people though, I think, is that our hearts tend to do a great job holding on to the horrible stuff and a horrible job holding on to the good. Or at least we're like that until we learn how to not be like that. But I hadn't learned that yet.

I was holding on so tightly to everything that had ever happened to hurt me. Daily, my mind would turn in circles, reliving moments that had cracked me wide open and left me feeling empty. It was this sort of devastating, destructive thinking that led me to bad coffee shops and beat-up books. I wanted to find out that this surface life I had been sold on was all a joke, that the deeper, more meaningful truth was right under my nose and all I had to do was sniff it out.

So I started seeking out something with depth: a defiant truth I could sink my desperate, disillusioned self into. Every single day I read books about things that I thought would lead me to blissful enlightenment—books about the present moment, about prayer, about belief, about healing. Truthfully, the books defied both my age and my intellect, but I read them with an unwavering determination rooted in both ambition and ignorance.

I wasn't raised religiously at all. I think my dad's religion was Molson Canadian, and I think my mother's was mainly ignoring my father's. There were two churches near my house, both of them run-down and unexciting. One of them, the United Church—which always seemed to have a broken back window—featured a new sign every month with some clever line about what God could do for your life. My personal favorite was BECAUSE THERE ARE SOME QUESTIONS GOOGLE CAN'T ANSWER. A runner-up was FAITHBOOK: GOD HAS SENT YOU A FRIEND REQUEST. Honestly, those both made me laugh, and I think laughter is as good an invitation to something as just about anything else. So I wasn't against religion, I had just never had any reason to be for it. Plus, Victoria is a pretty wide-open place spiritually.

Most people here do yoga and drink kale shakes and use words like *karma* and talk about the "law of attraction."

Not many people are into God. God sort of counters the paradigm that we control everything, which seems to be the preferred belief of a lot of people in Victoria and elsewhere. It's easier, I guess, to just ignore God than to debate him or his existence.

I didn't know much about what happened inside the walls of a church, but I knew that people who didn't go to church sure liked to argue with people who did. I wish there wasn't such a division between people who believe certain things and people who don't. It seems vastly hypocritical on both ends, these two groups of people both claiming to believe in good things and yet willing to do bad things to each other for disagreeing. That seems way wrong, or at the very least weird. I don't know a ton about Jesus or Buddha or Allah, but I think they would have been against casting one another out like that. That's part of the problem, too. The word *religious* has become a loaded gun of a word. It means so many different things to so many different people; ultimately, there is no way to know who is talking about what. It's a bunch of different interpretations to summarize a single idea—a single idea that no one seems to be able to agree on.

It seems like everyone just wants to argue about it. The addiction to being right is a nasty one. I almost always know I shouldn't care about being right, yet I invariably do. It's hard. I heard someone say one time that "anger after five seconds is just pride." Maybe when we become spiritual people, we become proud people. Or maybe we're all just angry at something, and talking about things that are impossible to prove is a good outlet for that anger. I don't know.

All I know is I kept reading my books. After a while, it started to dawn on me that they seemed to be almost the same, each floating in the same relative vagueness and generalities as the book before it. Words like "karmic destiny" and "divine creation" were littered throughout, and everyone seemed to talk about life as if it was this magical fairy tale that would bend to your every whimsical request. All you had to do was "set your intention" or "create a crystal-clear goal." It was all a bit annoying, really. But I just kept on following "the path," as these so-called gurus would describe it, hoping that if I just closed my eyes and kept my head down, either something good would happen or, at the very least, I wouldn't notice that the path was taking me right off a cliff. So every day, I woke up and I read a little bit more. I was unwavering in my habit, demolishing each book with a determination I didn't even know I had. The thing about committing to something is that once you're in, you're in. You start to drink a bit of the Kool-Aid and suddenly it seems just like tap water. To put it a bit more bluntly: you become weird. For me, my weirdness was expressed in more and more isolation.

· · ·

MY MIND STAYED stuck in my questions all fall, and my eyes stayed stuck in book after book. The days got darker earlier, and leaves fell on the ground. I went for walks and hid in my room.

My books kept me company and my fears kept me reading. Fall passed and winter finally showed up. The calendar flipped over to December, and all of a sudden the much-anticipated Christmas season was upon us. Well, much anticipated by everyone except me. Christmas always either pissed me off or put me in an irreversibly pessimistic headspace. My parents divorced during Christmas. I wonder if that's why it always brought up a lot of emotions for me, but I'm not sure. I don't even really remember being emotional when they broke up; it was hardly a surprise, after all. You know, sleeping in separate rooms and arguing and all that. So it wasn't as if one day we were posing for family photos in front of a snowman at a private ski resort and the next day my parents were splitting up and ruining my Christmas or something. I guess, more than anything, it seemed like at Christmastime I could always feel the harsh contrasts of the world.

My house on Hobbs was right near the end of the street. There was one more house before the stop sign, and then there was a crosswalk. If you crossed that crosswalk, you would be leaving Cadboro Bay and entering Queenswood. They were separated by about six inches of earth and about six figures of income. My friend Corey lived in the first house inside Queenswood. He was a funny guy who wore either sweatpants or two-thousand-dollar Hugo Boss jackets. He was almost twenty years older than I was and lived half the year in Los Angeles and half the year in Queenswood. We went to the same café and became friends more out of proximity than because of a fit of personality. Initially, it struck me as odd that a grown man who lived in one of the coolest cities in the world came home and stayed with his family for half the year. But that was before I met his family.

Corey's family was something out of a movie: extremely kind, good-looking, loving, and wealthy. It made me sick with jealousy. His house was enormous and elegant, always warm and well decorated and, during the holidays, home to a twelve-foot-tall Christmas tree with what seemed like hundreds of gifts underneath it. It reminded me of one of those massive displays in the mall windows where there are all these amazingly well-wrapped boxes tucked perfectly under the most lavish Christmas tree you've ever laid eyes on, as if to say, "Your Christmas won't be this good, but maybe if you work harder!" Only those boxes in the malls are empty and the ones at Corey's house were not. They were filled with expensive, shiny things that made a poor kid like me picture what it would be like to wake up there on Christmas morning, as if all my life problems could be solved perfectly by presents.

One night, after watching a rather lackluster movie at

Corey's house, while his family all went to bed, I walked around my neighborhood, staring up at the sky, trying to make sense of everything that seemingly lacked any logic. The cold was biting and the sky was so dark that it seemed like the stars were parked just a few feet above the street-lights. The wind was ripping through my skin, and it felt like the truth was ripping through my soul. It hit me, for the first time, that life is something of a constant duality, each moment capable of being pulled in any direction—good, bad, happy, sad. As much as I lusted after the life-style in that house in Queenswood, it dawned on me that so many people would lust after mine. If I kept walking and went fifteen minutes in the other direction—toward Pandora Street, where many of the homeless men and women of our city had carved out makeshift shelters for themselves on grassy medians—I could find someone who had much less than I did. And if I went another twenty minutes from Pandora, deep into the heart of the low-income housing of Quadra Village, I could find an entire family that barely had a roof over their heads, much less presents under the tree.

The whole thing seemed brutally cruel. Here I was, lost in my own selfishness of wondering who had a bigger house and better toys, and there were people sitting out in the cold with no food and no one to wish them a Merry Christmas—and, even if someone said the words, no real reason to believe them. How could we walk around spending money on gifts and toys for people who—much like us—didn't even really need them and not even fix this problem first? It seemed really wrong, and it made me feel destroyed inside. While I had never considered myself naïve, I was starting to wonder if I was.

The whole world wants to talk about happiness. Yet it seemed liked no one cared if it came at the cost of blindly ignoring hardship. How can you advocate for happiness without also advocating for equality? It was starting to feel to me like maybe all this stuff was just about money, and everyone was working their tail off marketing it as if it *wasn't* about money, so that you would buy their stuff and they would get rich and successful and buy shiny toys and tigers. Or whatever it is you do exactly when you make money like that. But this was when I really started to wonder how it is exactly we're supposed to be happy when the whole world seems to be bleeding out, hurt from the constant cuts of society's neglect and ignorance.

EVERYTHING THAT WINTER seemed to stand out, like I was noticing everything for the very first time. Nothing seemed whole anymore. The world looked like fragmented pieces of what used to be a complete picture but now was just a bunch of people standing around trying to fulfill their selfish desires.

It all made me really angry. All the books I had read

seemed good for nothing now. Was it a homeless person's "karmic destiny" to be living on the street? Was it a kid in Africa's "divine purpose" to be dirt poor? None of it was adding up. I couldn't live another second with all this suffering on my conscience, knowing I wasn't doing a damn thing about it.

I cried that Christmas. I quit eating meat and decided I was a vegetarian. I gave half my wardrobe away to a shelter. I told my mum that I wanted to only be a part of activities or sports where the purpose of playing was joy, not winning or losing. Winning or losing divides us, I declared to her decidedly. She smiled and told me I sounded like a "hippie from the seventies." I took that as a small compliment.

I wanted to radically change everything in my life. I wanted to give more and appreciate more and find a way to play a part in making the world and the people in it perfect. It was a small goal and I knew I could achieve it. I was determined to shrink this divide—the one between the oppressed and the oppressors, the haves and the have-nots, the get-to-sleep-in-a-beds and the make-a-bed-out-of-the-pavements—that seemed to be plaguing humanity and hurting so many people. I wanted to find a better way and then run to the top of a mountain and tell the world about it. It was a manic and mildly delusional moment all in one. With my newfound perspective, I felt excitement building up inside me like water behind a dam, ready to burst out into the world and flood the lives of men, women, and children with my formidable optimism. Finally, I felt like I had a reason to get out of bed in the morning.

It lasted for about three days.

Then suddenly Christmas was over. All the hype was gone, along with the high energy of the holiday season. All the mass commercialism and marketing I was so radically against disappeared. It was the New Year. People were hungover and tired and had spent too much money, and I was hungry from not eating meat and frustrated now having half the wardrobe I had had seventy-two hours before. In the moment it had felt good to give my things away, but now, sitting on my couch in a crappy T-shirt I had worn for three days straight, one that smelled like teenage body odor and regret, it felt like it was hardly enough. Here I was, showing up to a shelter and giving them clothes I'd sweated in, stained, and otherwise abused, and handing them off like they were the key to solving all the world's problems. Even more laughably, I was trying to cure my self-afflictions by passing off material possessions. Maybe that helps out a kid or two, but in the big picture it does nothing. My becoming a vegetarian—a whining, loud-mouth vegetarian, spewing facts about the food industry that I had memorized from a low-budget documentary— might impact the sales of one small grocery store, but that's it. In fact, it won't stop that store from continuing to order meat. And certainly it's a speck of dust in the wind of the larger issue. It wouldn't change anything at all. And it didn't. I just didn't have clothes. I just didn't eat meat. My "lifestyle changes," as I was committed to calling them, affected only me. My intention of being selfless had somehow reversed on me, illuminating both my ignorance and my inability to see outside myself, even when I was trying my hardest to do so. It was like the walls of reality were closing in upon my illusions, and all I could do was stand there and watch everything break into a million little pieces.

SOMEWHERE IN THERE, things changed. I lost the radical idealism. I stopped reading the spiritual books. I gave up on trying to ask the big questions. My life crawled back into the dimly lit corner it had worked so hard to come out of during these months. What was left was a heavy feeling of hopelessness; it was something I had never experienced. It was unshakable, as if it was in my skin and my bones and my breath. Everything I touched turned to more and more despair. The days became distant and hard to remember, and I felt almost always completely exhausted. I would roll around in my bed for hours every night, looking up at the ceiling and wondering when this would pass. My room became a hollowed-out shell of used food wrappers and old dishes and dirty clothes and broken possessions. Once my alarm clock went off for ten minutes without my turning it off, because in my coma-like slumber I didn't hear it. So my sister came into my room, turned it off, and on the way out managed to roll her ankle on one of the many glasses lying on the floor. It was embarrassing. But I had no idea what was happening or how to change it.

Every day seemed to stick to the day before it and the day after it, never separating itself enough to be memorable. And each moment that slipped out of my hands and into the echoes of yesterday, I was aware that my mind was stuck to the same thoughts and the same fear and the same hurt. Nothing was changing. In fact, things had gotten a whole lot worse.

I was ridiculously depressed and too dumb to even know it.

NOTE TO SELF

When you feel fucked up: Stop. Breathe. Talk to someone. Tell them stuff. Stop being an asshole and thinking you're going to get through it alone. Problems are like broken pipes: they need a person to fix them. Oh, and clean your room, you filthy animal.

7

Boy Meets Depression

IT TOOK ME months to realize that I was drowning in a deep and dark depression. It seems as though knowing you're depressed would be obvious—the way it is when you cut yourself or come down with a cold—but it isn't. It's as if suffering has a way of secretly finding a home inside of you, slipping past your own sense of self and common sense. I felt not unlike a ceiling with a tiny leak; water passed through me undetected, slowly flooding every inch of my existence.

I couldn't come to terms with the torture that I felt inside of me. It was as if I had become a stranger to myself, simply renting the skin of someone who looked familiar. It was haunting and horrible. Each day I felt like I was being dragged through life, clutching at anything and everything in hopes that if I could hang on to it, maybe it would make me feel normal again. Anything to do with emotion devastated me. I couldn't watch movies. I couldn't read books. I couldn't listen to music or make conversation. I fluctuated between being unbearably quiet and irrationally angry. Truly, I felt like I was losing my mind.

Pangs of pain and pessimism ran rampantly through my brain. I was angry and upset with who I was and what I thought about. I knew that no one could actually hear what happened in my mind but was horrified at the thought of what they'd hear if they could. This invisible playground where I was able to indulge in whatever whimsical version of the world I wanted to had turned into a battleground. It was the secrecy of the experience that made it so devastating. Slowly, the solitude of it all began to challenge my sanity.

On any average day, I was so lost in my own mind that there was nothing else that was real. Every conversation was like listening underwater. I could hear words and see gestures and make vague connections, but my focus, each and every conscious thought, was married to my sadness; nothing else successfully connected with me. It was pathetic and childlike, this compulsion to think only of myself, and yet it was unshakable. I hated that this was who I'd become. I felt less like a human being and more like a reaction. I flinched in the different directions of my despair and could not stand still long enough to notice I was doing it. Like a fish out of water, I jumped all over the place, trying to make it back to where it was safe while simultaneously exhausting myself.

At the end of some days, I noticed how much my shoulders had sunk in and my eyelids had drooped and how even my physical shell was telling me that I sucked. There was no lower level to sink to. This was rock bottom. My existence was no more than a meek, unremarkable puddle of jumping from painful thought to painful thought.

More time passed and I became more and more aware of how hard it was to get off this path. My mind was pulled toward only the ugliest, unbearable parts of being alive, as if toward a magnet. Obsessively, I alternated between thinking about what was wrong with people and thinking about what was wrong with myself; it was a Ping-Pong game that succeeded only in making everything shittier. Sometimes I took a pillow off my bed and put it in front of my face and tried to scream as loudly as I could. When I'm mad about something, this almost invariably works. But when I was in this tortured and tired state, it did nothing other than remind me how weak I was. I could barely bring myself to raise my voice a decibel above conversational level, and when I did finally guilt myself into producing something vaguely near a yell, it was short and insignificant and gave me little more than strained vocal cords. There was no satisfaction in it.

Every day was lost on me. I didn't count the days. I didn't care about them. In a weird way, depression had brought me to a place of extreme calm. Everything happened slowly. I was more aware than ever of just how much effort life takes. I lacked the willpower to care about anything. I had resigned myself to a life of pessimism. I readily expected the world to self-combust. Or at least, I readily expected myself to self-combust. It's hard to say whether or not I'd lost the desire to still be alive. But then again, something is only lost once you become aware it's gone missing. I was so deep into the darkness, I'd actually started to think that it was normal.

AS I TRIED my best to battle through this and through school, the thoughts in my head as I walked through the hallways each day ranged from "Fuck" to "Holy fuck" to "Was his hair pink?" to "I want to be invisible."

It was a weird mixture of emotions to live within. I was angry, aware, and exhausted all at the same time. Living with thoughts that run so rampantly and repetitively is hard. They start to dance circles around you, as if mocking you. I couldn't go more than a few seconds some days without thinking something that made me feel like an ant trapped in a jar. It was as if the whole world could see right through me to the deepest parts of my fear.

For the first time, I started to enjoy doing nothing: lying on the floor, my eyes staring at nothing but the ceiling, with all the lights out. This became almost blissful.

No one to bother me. No one to have to put on an act for. Just the room, me, and the dark. It felt familiar, like an old friend or a comfortable chair. I just sort of fell into it. I would lose hours of my life like this. Probably days. Just lying on the floor, looking up at the white paint on the low ceiling, counting the little black marks from the rubber of the weights that I used to lift. I had resigned myself to being this person now, one who was attached to the floor and tried to daydream his problems away. It was pitiful, and made worse by my being hell-bent on telling no one about just how bad it really was.

That's part of the thing about depression and feeling broken—you just swim in shame all day long. Now I was too tired to keep on swimming, though. Now I felt like my head was going under and I was running out of air and the ambition to keep on going. As I lay there, I wondered if it was possible to sink any further than this while still having a heartbeat. I tried to think back to something happy or joyful or amazing, and while I could successfully pull at a memory, I couldn't come close to accessing the emotions. I was losing the ability to even live inside my own daydreams. Where I once was the main character, able to carefully feel every moment of my memories, I was now just a limp observer, standing on the sidelines, watching, wondering if life would ever feel good again.

• • •

SOMETIMES I THINK of my depression as a fog. I grew up by the water, and so many early mornings of my childhood began with waking up to fog. In a way, fog is both beautiful and haunting at the same time. It's hard to define, hold, or interact with, and yet it exists. It's there. You can't really clear it away just because you want it to be gone. At the same time, you always know that the fog is just temporary. It's always just rolling through. It will be here for a while and then it will pass. And eventually it will disappear completely and the world as you know it will come back into plain view, like it never even left. But in the meantime, while it's still hanging in the air as thick as smoke, you can't see life the way you used to see it. The beauty is missing and the perspective is gone. You can only see the six inches in front of your face, and those six inches aren't pretty; they're all out of focus, blurry.

That's how I feel about my depression sometimes: that I'm living inside the fog. Hoping that when it lifts—if it lifts—life will look the same as it did before it started.

I've lived in the fog a lot. It changes and it bends and it finds a new way to creep up on you, but its essence, its misery, its weight, remain the same. The really scary part about being depressed is the duration. A few days and it's hard; it hurts, but you can persevere through it. It's when it shows up for more than a few days—when it turns into weeks—that is where it gets scary. It gets scary mainly because you begin to think it's normal, how life is and will continue to be.

By nature, I want people to think that I'm more complete than I am, so when depression shows up I have the habit of pretending that everything is fine. You tell people everything is fine, and slowly you start to believe yourself and that this is the way to live. You've been in the fog so long you've forgotten about the life you led up to that point.

All you can see is the moment you're stuck inside.

One of my friends who watches a lot of fringe documentaries and spends too much time on the Internet told me about this sort of bro-science, New Age psychological study where they put a bunch of goldfish in a bowl and they put a glass wall in the middle of the bowl. At first the fish think they can swim past it. But then they hit their heads on the glass and realize that they're wrong. Eventually all the fish learn they can't swim past it; every single fish adapts and changes. None of them run into the glass again. Then after another week, the people take the glass out of the water. I'm not sure if fish can see or can process things like that, as most of my personal experience underwater has been in community pools where there is a noticeable absence of sea creatures, but the fish stay in the tank the whole time it's being removed. When the glass is out and there's no longer a limitation in their environment—other than the tank itself—none of the fish swim past where the glass used to be. They're so adjusted to their situation that they don't even notice it's changed.

I don't know if that's a real study, but I really hope it

is. My friend talks about weird stuff like this all the time, and I tend to nod and smile and then wonder whether or not he's doing okay. But if it is a real study, it's one of the most accurate metaphors for living in the fog that I've ever heard. Because once you start believing in the glass, it's hard to know whether you believe it because it's real or it's real because you believe it. That's when things start to get a bit messy.

THE MORE YOU get lost in the darkness of your own depression, the more it feels ridiculous to ask for help. For me, I start to tell myself untrue things and then believe them. The lies start out smallish: *You suck. You're ugly. No one thought your bike was cool when you were a kid.* Those sorts of things. But then they get bigger. *You're not important. You don't matter. This is how you're going to feel forever.* And you start to believe it because you're stuck.

Being stuck is shitty. It feels persistent, permanent. Like your life is wading through wet concrete and you're standing there, defenseless, feeling it dry. You don't have to get encased in this. Really, there are only a handful of ways to lift yourself an inch off the ground when you're truly depressed, and all of them have to do with talking to other humans, which, quite unsurprisingly, is the exact dead last thing you want to do.

There's no particularly fun way to talk about being depressed.

At first you don't want to because it's like picking at the cut you've already been picking at for the last six hours and now inviting others to pick at it as well. It feels redundant and painful. So you tell yourself that your living in isolation benefits both you and everyone else. It's a nice, albeit false, moral ground to attempt to stand on for a while. Then it becomes more about the guilt.

I've always felt a bit guilty about being depressed. Mainly because I feel like I don't have one good reason to feel the way I do. So you want to hide the truth to spare yourself the agony of facing certain questions. The ones that hit deep and close to home. Everyone wants to know "why" you're depressed. We like logic, I guess. If you're hurt, something has to have hurt you. If you're sad, something made you sad. But sometimes when you're living inside of your own depression, asking what caused it is like asking what causes a car engine to turn on. It's not one thing. It's a collection of things together, so interwoven that it becomes nearly impossible to separate one from the other.

You're entangled in a puzzle, and you can't see a single piece as separate; it's just a part of the same plague that persistently pushes you underneath the current of your own happiness. This can make it even harder to feel like your depression is justified. When there's nothing to point to and blame, we tend to just blame ourselves. That's when the downward spiral really starts to happen. My downward spiral looks a lot like this:

I'm depressed.
Why am I depressed?
I don't know.
This is bullshit.
I'm still depressed.
This is still bullshit.
Why am I depressed?
Have I showered?
I haven't showered.
I fucking stink.
Why am I depressed?
I have nothing to be depressed about. I'm so ungrateful;
     there are kids dying of cancer and I'm existentially
     upset over nothing.
I'm a bad person.
Typo: I'm the worst person ever.
I'm still depressed.
I'm still depressed.
Why isn't anything changing?!!?
I'm still depressed.

It sort of just continues like this until I run out of energy or creative ways to make myself feel like crap.

That's a lot of what depression is: trying to make yourself feel worse while other people try to make you feel better. It's unbelievably kind of anyone to reach out to someone who is dealing with these sorts of feelings. Generally speaking, depressed people make absolutely awful friends/company/humans. They don't want to talk. Or smile. Or laugh. Or eat. Or do anything that involves physical movement or joy. You really have to be a saint to put up with someone in this frame of mind. You're basically saying you just appreciate that person for continuing to stay alive. At that moment, doing so is a legitimate, hard-earned victory.

Not losing the will to live in a season of dark depression is the single most important—and most challenging—thing. Of course it sounds so simple. The idea of not wanting to live seems borderline offensive to some. I get that. To a person who maybe has never felt the feelings that depression can bring—the ones that make you feel as though you're flattened, anguished, alone—or contemplated the idea of suicide, it might not make a whole lot of sense.

But depression has this way of deflating you over time. It pulls all the passion and purity out of you like a ball losing air. It's slow and gradual. But eventually you wake up and you've lost all the parts of you that made you who you are. Suddenly you're just trapped in your own body and your own bad beliefs, and you lack the perspective to pull it back together.

To me, depression isn't an emotion. Emotions are mostly fleeting and brought on by just cause. Emotions you can just push off to the side. Ask any guy who has ever been sad and then has been offered sex. He gets unsad

pretty freaking quick. But depression is different. It's a lens
to see life through. It's clouded; tinted with negativity. Everything you look at through this lens becomes warped
and out of whack with reality.

For me, there were times of such unexplainable angst
that it seemed like everything I was capable of thinking
had to be among the worst things ever thought by a human
being. I can distinctly remember seeing a mother hug her
child and thinking, "That kid is going to die one day."
I didn't mean it in a malicious way. Certainly, I had no
plans to force said death upon her, as I was too depressed
to even get close to a human being and likely lacked the
physical strength to do damage to a juice box much less
any vital arteries. But it was a thought I had, one that was
morbid and irregular, but that I noticed didn't really freak
me out. The frequency with which my mind crawled into
deep and dark places had increased so much I was almost
immune to it.

Because that is where your mind starts to go when
you're depressed—into the darkest nooks and crannies
of the human spirit. You just feel completely stuck there,
unable to move. The projections of your own bitterness
and anger start to become the thoughts you have, which
start to become the actions you take. And the actions you
take become the life you lead, and it all starts to become
one big gerbil wheel of disillusionment and pain and that
nasty, dirty word: *depression*.

. . .

WHEN THINGS WERE really bleak and brutal, I became a shell of myself, one encased in self-pity and pessimism. Nothing made sense to me anymore. I could find the flaws in absolutely anything, and I dove headfirst into hating the whole world. I stopped talking to people. I didn't change my clothes. I once didn't eat for two days. Not because I didn't have food. I did. But instead it was because I came to the rather innovative conclusion that there truly was no point in eating. Ultimately, I would just have to eat again. No matter what I did or what I chose to believe or do or say, I was permanently in debt to my stomach and my own need for survival. I could make the best pasta in the whole world and spend hours seasoning it, preparing it, draining it, and putting it in my favorite bowl with my favorite fork, and it would be good. But then, no matter what I did, in a few hours I would just be hungry again. And I would have to start all over. Only this time it would be worse. Because now I would have less food and more dishes that needed to be done. So if anything, eating would have me putting myself backward.

These were the thoughts that made me starve for forty-eight hours straight.

This type of thinking is why, over time, you start to feel like you're truly going crazy. What's going on in your head is not logical, rational, or, quite frankly, remotely intelligent. It's all just gibberish, scattered, fractured, non-sensical arguments of anguish that you've blended into a narrative of unbeatable negativity. You're creating a story of why life is bad and then retelling it to yourself every single day. It's like self-hypnosis for people who want to hate themselves.

The tricky part is that at the very beginning, you sort of know the story you're telling yourself is just a story. You know you're not in a good place and that's why you're thinking bad things. You know your thoughts aren't what they normally are, and you might even be aware that you're not in a healthy headspace. But then time passes and things don't change and so you start to slip a little deeper into the fog. Things get a little less clear. It happens gradually, the way ice melts into a drink. Before long you start to believe the story you've been telling yourself just a little bit more. The voice in your head that says this is all going to pass starts to get a bit quieter. And that other voice in your head—the one that insists on lying to you—starts to tell you that this is how it is. It starts to tell you, "This is your life and it really does suck as much as you think it does." Now what was once just a story starts to become more and more like scripture. You're swimming so deep in the lies, you don't even remember the truth anymore. In an instant you've lost your sense of self and replaced it with a sense of hopelessness and pain.

Everything only gets harder from there.

It's harder to wake up at a reasonable hour. It's harder to talk to anyone. It's harder to remember to take showers. Yes, you will need to remember to shower. Cleaning your body goes to the bottom of the priority list pretty quickly when your brain starts to tell you that life is a waste of time. Everything gets more difficult. You eat less. You sleep more but less restfully. You turn your phone off and ignore calls, and then get anxiety about not getting back to people. You forget what it feels like to sweat. You hit the Mute button on your life, and everything fades to black.

This is the point where things become really scary and shaky. The truth is, you probably no longer have the optimism required to create a change in your life; you lost it to the fog. So now you're dependent on someone else, or something else, to help you reassemble the fragments of your life. But you're shutting everyone out. Your vision is so clouded by your own self-loathing that even if God himself came down and spoke to you, handed you a personalized note of encouragement on fully customized letterhead, signed by a dozen angels, you would likely write it off as a coincidence. So now you're all alone on an island that only you know how to get to. And you burned all the boats.

What happens next is never anything good. Things start to slip: relationships, time, meaning. Pain becomes much easier to feel than hope. Getting rid of the hurt takes priority over healing, even though it seems like the two would be interlinked. But they're not. Because when you're deep in the dark hole of depression and wanting to get rid of the hurt, you look not toward getting help but toward getting rid of yourself. That's when the suicidal thoughts start to emerge. At least, that's when they did for me.

It's not that you want to die. No one really does, I don't think. I certainly never did. It's just that you have no more will to live. Life has become a pointless, futile affair of meaningless exchanges of energy and ideas that ultimately perpetuate your own solitary identity and confinement to your own angry, awful consciousness. And you want no part of it anymore. You're tired. This constant effort is exhausting. You just want to detach from the soul of this self-inflicted suffering and be free. And there seems to be only one way to do that: getting rid of your pulse.

For me, the thoughts started slowly. Very slowly, in fact. The first one was actually a bit of a release. I was sixteen, maybe seventeen. It was in the summer. I was standing by an apple vendor at an outdoor market with people milling about everywhere trying to negotiate deals on fruit or lamps or eccentric blankets made by hippies. Lots of people were high. Everyone seemed so happy. I was not savvy enough to realize that the former was influencing the latter. The sun was shining down. The sky was blue. The ocean was our neighbor. And joy seemed to be living inside of everyone. If energy is ever contagious, on that day I certainly felt immune. Everyone was happy and I hated myself. It hurts to have other people's joy be a mirror to your own pain. It really hurts. As I stood there, trying to distance myself from my own emotions, a little thought danced into my head. It said: "Well, if this is really so bad, you could always just kill yourself."

I had never thought that before. Of course, I knew what suicide was. I knew people died by suicide. I just had never thought about suicide for myself. I had never seen it as a plan or a possibility. But then the thought showed up that summer day, and the weirdest thing happened: I felt better. Not a ton better. But a little better. A bit lighter, almost. It was like a little drug hit of total calm. I hadn't experienced peace like that in forever, it felt like. I wasn't sure what it was about that thought that made me feel better. It just did. Maybe it was the idea that escape was always possible. That freedom could be just around the corner. That was how it started.

From there, the thought only grew bigger. Almost every time I would find myself in a moment that was becoming too excruciating to bear, I would bring myself back to this thought: "Well, I could always just kill myself." It would invariably give me the same short-lived feeling of calm. Pretty quickly, I was addicted to that feeling of peace and subsequently to the thought that was responsible for it. It went from once a month, to once a week, to once a day, to three or four times every single day. It was the crack cocaine of addictive thoughts. And suddenly, I was a full-blown addict, pulling myself through life for the twisted pleasure that came with the idea of no longer being here.

Mostly the thought showed up when I was weak and hurting. I would be alone in my room or standing out on the street late at night and I would think about death; turning it over and over in my mind, touching its edges and intricacies.

The idea of not being alive was becoming my light at the end of the tunnel. It made the darkness of where I was so much more bearable. To know that it could all be over was such an amazing feeling at that time. It gave me certainty in a time when everything felt deeply uncertain, shaky. These are some of the places that you can get taken to when you're depressed and discouraged, stuck squarely in the middle of everything that is heavy, harsh, and hurtful.

Even though I struggle/fight/deal with depression, I would like to make it blatantly clear that even I think it's kind of ridiculous.

Look: I grew up in a decent neighborhood. We were dysfunctional and I didn't really know much of my father besides his drinking and I got bullied a bit, but still . . . if I can speak completely objectively, I didn't have it *that* hard. I mean, I went around with a UNICEF box on Halloween. I wasn't the recipient of the UNICEF box.

Plus, how can anyone be depressed as a teenager? What did I have to be depressed about? My lack of responsibility and how my age removed me from almost all consequences, both legally and morally? It's a bit absurd really. Here I was hating my life and being depressed, and that wasn't even close to the worst part. The worst part was that I hated myself for it, and it made me feel like an idiot. Well, maybe not an idiot. But at the very least an ungrateful shit.

One of my teachers in elementary school, Mrs. Mathers, a kind woman who wore the largest pair of glasses I had ever seen on a person's face, used to say to us, "You have nothing to be sad about. Kids in Africa, they have something to be sad about." She would go on and on like this, describing in painstaking detail the depths of what life looked like there, a place she had quite naturally never been. All of us kids would just kind of nod, as if we fully understood the weight of the turbulent situations, civil warfare, and political corruption happening halfway across the world. She talked about Africa as if we all had been there on a field trip and seen these things firsthand instead of as a part of the planet we couldn't even find on a map. We were six. I think she was maybe just talking out loud to practice her arguments or something. As I got older, though, it seemed like people always had one of these lines ready to make your problems seem insignificant.

"At least you're not starving."

"At least you have shelter."

"At least you only got caught masturbating once."

Okay, maybe no one said that last one. But people would say stuff like this all the time, as if their verbal shaming somehow helped all the starving, homeless, devastated kids in the world. As much as I despised this kind of "be grateful" sermon, I see how they are completely right. I *am* lucky to have what I have. I'm incredibly, indescribably lucky for absolutely all of those things. I'm completely aware that my birth, my arrival in a First World country with health care, is absolute luck courtesy of the ovarian lottery. It has nothing to do with me—not in the slightest. I didn't "deserve" it. I didn't earn it. I didn't get it because I'm a good person. I didn't even choose it. It's absolute blind chance where you end up in this world, and who is going to be responsible for raising you and feeding you and making sure you don't sleep in dirt. And I got lucky. I get all that. I really do.

But I also get that sometimes I wake up in a world that seems completely confusing, terrorizing, and morally bankrupt. And I have felt that way since I was old enough to think, and the feelings only seem to intensify with time. So while I can't ignore my gratefulness, I also can't ignore the reality I experience and encounter every day.

And that's where the whole depression thing really kicks in.

I get depressed. I can admit this. It happened a lot back then and happens semi-frequently today, and it doesn't do much explaining when it arrives. It just sort of shows up and hangs around for a bit. Sometimes a day. Sometimes a week. Sometimes until I stare at myself in the mirror and scream. It's all a bit of a mystery to me. What worked yesterday might not work again today. What works today might not work tomorrow. It's a high-stakes guessing game, with no rule book and no guidelines. You just wake up and suddenly you're back inside of it, wondering how it was exactly that you got out of it last time.

What it feels like to be depressed is a small dose of insanity. It's a looming, disturbing, anxiety-ridden realization that life feels hopeless and you don't know how to fix it. That's the real tough part to take: you're broken and you don't know how to fix it. You're just feeling this . . . thing. It just sort of sits somewhere inside and irritates you until the most joyous of moments morph into boring milliseconds of life being wasted before we die. It's absolutely horrifying to see how fast your mind can switch from moments of magic and joy into that place of darkness and despair. Life loses its meaning in all of a minute, and you spend the rest of your time trying to find it again.

Perhaps the more horrifying part is not knowing whether the place you find yourself in is a lie; maybe it's the truth, and we just get good at distracting ourselves from it. I've thought about a lot when I'm depressed, and sometimes things make more sense than when I am happy. When you're happy you're sort of just like a drunk person. You're agreeable and easy to talk to and you don't really need things explained to you. Everything is easy and you can just go with the flow. You don't need to ask questions. You don't need to get answers. You just exist. You just live. Things make sense. And if they don't, you're okay with that, too.

When you're depressed, you want to watch life through every different camera angle that exists and then rewind the film and ask yourself why everything just sucks so damn much. Then you do that a couple hundred times in a day and eat a cheeseburger and turn your phone off and then turn it on again. Maybe you make it out of your sweatpants if you're ambitious. If depression was a drug, it would not need to be illegal because no one would buy it. You can't sell people on an unexplainable, existential crisis that questions every inch of their character. It just doesn't have much cachet to it.

LUCKILY, MY DEPRESSION has always passed. It takes time and it never leaves as fast as I would like it to. But it passes. Depression really is an emotional kick in the balls. And anyone who has ever been kicked in the balls can tell you, it doesn't matter whether the pain lasts for ten seconds or ten minutes—you'd just rather not have been kicked in the balls. Life just would have been better that way.

Depression conflicts with society's lens. Pretty much

everything you could ever see in an ad or a subway station billboard contradicts the idea of depression. I think maybe we want the life that is pitched to us by car companies and clothing brands. Maybe we want everything to have a quick fix, a happy ending, and a smiling child. I think we want to believe life should just be a dream. That is so simple. Work, buy some stuff, work some more, buy some more stuff, get a hot wife, get a shiny car, put the hot wife in the shiny car, and show your not-shiny-car-driving, not-hot-wife-having peers how well you did in life. That's the recipe. That's what we're sold on. But being depressed doesn't really fit anywhere in that narrative. So we develop seemingly different explanations for it.

The church might call depression a spiritual sickness. The aboriginal community a few hundred miles from where I live would tell you it's a demon. The doctor might tell you it's a disease. And almost everyone else will just tell you to stop being soft and lazy—as if your brokenness is nothing more than an excuse for bad behavior.

My stance is that it's potentially all of the above.

Have I been depressed before because I had no sense of self? Yes. Have I felt like a demon is possessing me? Sort of. But I was on mushrooms. Do I think I have a disease? No. But neither does someone who can't stop hoarding coupons. Do I think when I'm depressed I need to just stop being weak and weird? Only every single time. Does that ever really work? No. Not even once.

So what is depression? What is the fog? You start to sound like a crazy person just describing the thing that makes you feel crazy. Pitching people who have never personally experienced depression or loved anyone struggling with it is somewhere in the same ballpark as pitching people on fringe religions. You sound strange, almost detached from reason or rational thought, like a small child who is shouting strings of syllables in a desperate attempt to be understood. Certainly, diving deep into your cultural viewpoints on depression is not the most potent pickup approach at a party.

We have no idea how many people experience depression. Sure, you can do research and studies and go walk up to a million and one people in a Starbucks and ask them if they ever get depressed, but how do we really know what they mean by their answers? A lot of people would just say no whether that's the truth or not. No one wants to admit to being depressed because it sounds terrible, weak, ungrateful. Fill in the blank. But that's because it *is* terrible. Yet how can *anyone* say that he never wakes up and feels this way? Can you walk around the world and see the same things I see and not *ever* be depressed? Not even for a minute or an hour or a day? And if so, how? Maybe you have to just ignore the world to feel good. Maybe it's that simple. But I don't know.

I mean, how can you just meditate the day away when you know that kids are getting killed and people are dying from diseases we probably have the cure to and husbands are cheating on their wives and the world is basically melting morally? How do you find inner peace with that situation? I don't quite get it. Yet I can't stop thinking about it sometimes. I know I shouldn't be so obsessive about it and have pretty much nothing to offer to help as I am basically just a small pawn in the grand scheme of life, but it still eats at me. There's so much horror and inequity and disparity, and yet we all just find a way to make ourselves comfortable with it.

People seem deep when they say "not to worry about things that you can't control." It sounds really smart, but maybe it's also just selfish. It makes us feel better about being lazy. It's about comfort, not truth. We want to be able to sleep at night. I want to be able to sleep at night, too. But not because I sweep the shitty parts of my life under the rug and then make sure I never look down. That's not enlightenment. I think that's just procrastination.

EVERYTHING GOT WORSE around winter. It had been almost a full year since my experimental, albeit unsuccessful, attempt at self-discovery, and I was feeling heavy and hopeless all over again. The holiday blues started to wash over me, and everything was colder and more miserable than the month before. For a few days, it would feel as if my depression was lifting. I would wake up with energy and a clear head. It felt great and was a refreshing change from the monotony of my usual days. But every time it felt like the tide was turning, it wouldn't. After a few days of calm, I would wake up right back in the thick of it. Some days were so bad, I would pin my bedsheet over my window and sleep till noon. Avoiding the glaring eyes of the world outside, I would try to close my eyes and pretend everything was going to be perfectly all right. It rarely worked, and more and more, I just felt exhausted. Physically, emotionally, mentally. I was wiped out. Fighting the fog every day and afraid to tell anyone or talk about it. My life was rapidly becoming a nightmare.

It was around then that the suicidal urges started to creep back in. While they had never really left, it had felt like they had taken a long sabbatical. It had been months since I had last heard the cold, chaotic knock of those thoughts at my door. Suddenly, they were right there, begging to be let back in. The thoughts were always small whispers, yet carried the same feeling of relief as when I had first entertained them. Thinking about this all being over was the only thing that gave me any strength to keep moving forward.

Christmas came and went. The presents were opened and then closed, and the whole thing went off without much drama or excitement. Then the New Year snuck around and people were more excited for a bit. Everyone has a plan in the New Year. No one really follows through on that plan, it seems, but everybody starts with one. My plan was that if life wasn't better in a year, I was going to kill myself. It seemed more logical than it sounds now; I really, truly believed this was the only exit plan there was from my penetrating, persistent pain. I was going to give life twelve months to give me a reason to stay alive, or I was going to do the opposite.

Turns out, a year is a long time to wait. It took me only a month and some change before I decided I couldn't take it any longer. The days were all blending into one never-ending loop of loneliness and internal dialogue. My mum kept asking me if I was okay, and I kept lying and telling her yes. She was so kind and loving that I couldn't imagine hurting her, and I was so lost in my own pain, I couldn't see that lying to her was doing just that. Everything seemed like a waste, as if we were all just trying to keep ourselves busy to avoid facing the fact that we were all headed for a sweeping end. We were all going to die, and I was the only one smart enough to speed up the process. Everything else was a joke.

This was my last year of high school. All my friends kept talking about what college classes they were going to take or what apprenticeship program they were going to audit. It all made me sick. I wanted to grab them by the shoulders and give them a shake and scream out, "WHO CARES?!" I was so angry and infuriated that I was the only one intellectual enough to realize how dumb this life, this existence, this world really was.

Everyone basically just wants to be loved and not be lonely, and those two things are often translated through sex. Sex leads to babies. Babies lead to kids. Everyone in my school—everyone in my life—was just a result of two people who wanted to bang. That was it. And here we are, walking around as if it all matters, as if it's important what job we have or how much money we're able to accumulate and stuff inside our pockets. I had made up my mind, and my mind said none of this stuff mattered. It was all just a distraction. A way to keep people on the hamster wheel, hopelessly spinning their way toward a tomorrow that they think will magically be better than today. It's all just a way to keep us from facing the ugly truth that we don't have a clue what's going on. I didn't want to distract myself anymore. I just wanted it to be over.

The end of February is a strange time of year. It's still winter, but it's also almost spring. There are no leaves on the ground and no flowers either. It's a time of change. That was true for me that year.

If you read any books about addiction or recovery, there's a common line that says everyone needs to find his "bottom." A bottom is just the moment when everything hits you all at once, I guess. It's a lot like it sounds, but everyone's bottom is different. That's another thing they say in books about this stuff—that no two bottoms are the same. I guess it makes sense. If no two people are the same, then how could their moments of awakening be? I always wondered, though, how people end up as addicts. I watched my dad growing up, and I always wondered why he didn't just stop. I mean, I know he liked to drink and drinking helped him like himself, but when stuff was really going bad and he was losing his marriage and his kids and his life, why didn't he just stop? It seemed so obvious. All he had to do was change. Too bad I gave advice better than I followed it. At the time, wearing pajamas and sleeping in till the afternoon, I didn't realize that hidden in plain sight of my own two eyes, I was on a fast track to my own bottom.

If you were able to fly back in time to February 26 in Victoria, you would see and feel a few different things. There was a soft blanket of snow sitting atop the ground, something that was out of the ordinary but welcome. The air was dry and harsh, so cold it cut right through you. The tree branches, normally softly swaying in the wind, were now heavy and barely able to hold themselves up. My feet crunched when I walked and my ears burned bright red, sensitive to the frigid winter air that we normally didn't encounter in our coastal climate. But it would be a pretty ordinary scene. I didn't know it then, but that day would be anything but ordinary for me.

I had the house to myself. My mum and sister were out of town together, and I was the only one to look after the place. I got home late in the evening, coming home from a friend's house where I had briefly stopped off. It was too alive, too euphoric for my emptiness. When I came in the door, the house was dark and freezing cold enough for me to think that every window in the house had been left open. They hadn't been, but I checked to be sure. I cranked the heat and went downstairs to my room. The house that night was the quietest it has ever been. If you closed your eyes, you could hear your own heartbeat. I had a half-empty bottle of vodka in my room and a pen and paper. It was so silent, it was like the walls were trying to listen. If they could have, they would have heard a teenage kid hit rock bottom.

That night, sitting in the bedroom that my father used to litter with beer cans and that I had since reclaimed, I put pen to paper and wrote out my suicide note. It started with a simple apology to my mum and my sister. I knew it was going to suck for them. They really did love me and I really did love them, but for whatever reason, that just wasn't enough. I thought about doing it somewhere else— like a cliff or a building or something—but I didn't want them to think I had gone missing. I figured that would be harder on them. So, in an effort to make something awful slightly less anguishing, I decided it was best just to do it here in my room. It was hard to think about how it would affect them. As much as I had struggled, my mum and sister were the only thing I knew that was true; they provided a constant sense of closeness and connection. I felt like I was letting them down. Probably because I knew that I was.

So I started the note with an apology. It was long-winded, wrought with the shame of not ever letting them inside behind the walls to know and see who I really was. Then I started to explain myself. I talked about the pointlessness of this whole thing we call life. I talked about how I hated my own selfish nature and that I made myself sick with my self-obsession. I wrote about how I hadn't had a real friend since Jordan died. I wrote about how I felt like no one knew me. I wrote about how I didn't even know myself. In a raging fury, I wrote for a half hour straight. Everything just bled out onto the page. It was like I vomited all my worst fears about life in black ink. When my wrist hurt from scribbling and my mind hurt from thinking, I finally stopped. It was long and double-sided and barely legible. I worried that maybe I should rewrite it so that it would be easier to understand. Seemed like it would suck not to be able to read something as permanent as a suicide note properly.

But there was no more time for editing at that point. I decided against the rewrite and leaned back against the wall of my room. The vodka bottle was still calling me to make it completely empty, but I ignored it. I was too far into my own head to think about anything other than what I was thinking about. So I just sat there. The plan

had been to swallow a whole bottle of pills. Somewhat embarrassingly, I wasn't even sure if that would actually work,
which added to my nervousness. Throughout the night, I
felt this creeping sensation; it was stronger than shame, but
weaker than full-on self-hatred. I knew this whole thing
was wrong. Every impulse of it felt wrong, dirty, disgusting. When I had previously considered the ending of my
own life, it had somehow seemed beautiful. Artistic, even.
Sort of like a tortured soul staking his one claim to control. Showing the world, in a giant "fuck you," that I could
do whatever I wanted to do. But now, sitting there, staring
at my note, exhausted by the emptiness of both my room
and my life, there was nothing remotely beautiful about
it. It was dark. Gross. A few times, I tried to think about
what it would feel like to be unburdened of my pain; how
the last moments might feel as my mind slipped from consciousness and my body went numb . . . and the feeling I
found so alluring, of being alleviated from my anguish,
would wash over me. But I couldn't feel it. All I could
feel was this boiling, brash sense of betrayal. Sure, I was
betraying my family and my friends. But deeper than that,
I felt I was betraying myself. That, underneath it all, I was
afraid. So afraid, in fact, that I would rather stop breathing, stop being alive, than face my fears. It was a haunting thought that I knew was true. This wasn't about being
"strong." This wasn't an attempt at heroics. It wasn't proving anything to anyone. What washed over me instead in

the midst of this thinking was powerful: that maybe I was more than what I had ever given myself credit for.

For so long, I had been convinced that my pain, my depression, my fears, were bigger than I was. That depression was the sky and I was merely a small cloud. And now, I wondered if maybe it was the other way around. That maybe depression lived inside of me and not me inside of it. I had been running so long that I wasn't sure what would happen if I were to simply stop. But on the other hand, I could feel this pulsing, vibrating truth: that I was more than my meekness. And that perhaps these pills, this plan, this note, this moment, this horrifying, hard BOTTOM, was the invitation to realize that.

I knew then that I could not do it. I could not kill myself. Fuck, I wanted to. I wanted nothing more than for the pain to end, the pressure to be relieved. But I knew I couldn't do it. It took me many more hours—long, heavy hours—to fully accept that death was not going to be my saving grace. That I was going to have to be.

I sat in my room and I cried. No, perhaps cried is not accurate. You cry when you get a bad cut or an injury or you care about something or someone that no longer cares about you. This was much worse, much more weighted, than that. It was a coming undone. Exhaustion, regret, anger, loathing. All just leaked out of me. It was a marathon of my worst moments, and at the end of it, I was empty. Only this time, I was not empty in the way I had once felt but in a way that I knew I was done fighting. I was done trying to torture myself. I was now empty in the kind of way that gives you space to fill yourself back up.

I'm not sure how much time passed. It might have been an hour, it might have been five. I really have no idea. But I know that I sat there, soaking in the silence, listening to my heart pound out of my chest, and I let go of all the things I had been holding on to so tightly. Then I picked up the note again. And that's when I realized I had it all wrong.

Putting those words on the page to explain why I was ending my life is unquestionably the very thing that saved it. For the first time, all this stuff wasn't just somewhere inside of me. It was out. It was on this piece of paper. That one piece of paper had seventeen years of secrets and shame on it. And it hit me right then that this piece of paper was just a story. It was just a story. And like any story, it needed an ending. But this was the wrong ending. I was choosing a bad ending to punish myself for a bad beginning. But I didn't choose the beginning. I could only choose how to change from this moment forward. I couldn't change the other stuff. I couldn't fix any of it. But I could fix this. I could just stop right here, right now, and start over.

I started to cry once more, this time lighter. I felt like I got it now. My problem this whole time wasn't anything other than myself. I was too proud to admit I was imperfect and too scared to say I had secrets. I cried off and on all night. Somewhere in there, my eyes stopped staying open and I fell asleep. The light to my room was still on, and the letter I had so furiously written still lay on the floor. It took me almost twenty full hours to wake up, and when I did, I wondered if it had all been a dream, a memory of a moment of madness.

Almost killing yourself and then not doing so is a hard-to-define experience. On one hand, nothing really happened that night. I sat alone in my room, I wrote some stuff down on a piece of paper, and I thought about ending my life. Thought about it to the point of mental and physical exhaustion. But I didn't do it. The whole thing felt surreal, as if it didn't truly happen. Truthfully, I think I was still in shock. It took me a long time to tell anyone at all about that night. Mainly because I realized it made me sound at best insane and at worst a liar in need of attention.

So I told no one and carried on with my life.

The thing is, though, almost ending your own life changes the way you see the rest of your life. It's not as simple as just waking back up, taking a shower, putting on a clean T-shirt, and continuing on. You start to see some depth where you never saw it before. Things seemed more fragile. I saw other people's brokenness more clearly, and it hit harder than before. Ironically, I started to appreciate my own life, the one riddled with problems and pain and imperfections. Things started to shift for me.

I told my mum about it. I've never seen her cry like that. It was hard, but I knew it was healthy. It felt so freeing to not live in the shadows anymore. I felt like I was coming out of the closet or something. The whole thing was refreshing and redemptive. I had almost killed myself. I came within inches and then I didn't. It had happened in the dead of night, with no witnesses, and yet it had been the single most defining moment of my life.

No one knew anything was different, and I didn't know if anything would ever be the same.

NOTE TO SELF

Sometimes you need to go into the dark to be able to appreciate the light. Other times you're really darkly, dangerously depressed and need to deal with it. You need to know the difference. If you can't tell, talk to someone. Now. And remember: no one ever lived an epic life by sleeping all day, worrying all night, and being too afraid to tell anyone about his problems.

8

Leather Chairs in Sooke

SOMEWHERE IN ALL this, my mother started convincing me I should go to counseling. I was as resistant to the idea as you would probably expect a seventeen-year-old boy to be and did my best to ignore the subject whenever it came up. She tried to convince me I needed counseling, and I tried to convince her I did not; and like most arguments with the person who created you, you do not end up winning.

So my mum started trying to find counselors for me and I just continued to pretend I was going to have a say in the matter. The truth was, I probably could have avoided going to counseling if I really, really wanted to put up the fight. I had this sort of knack for using my tongue to create tiny little cracks in situations—ones so small you could barely notice them, but still big enough for me to slip right through them. But there was this big part of me that knew I should go. I knew I should go and I wanted to go; I just wanted to go under the pretense that I was angry about the whole thing and it sucked. The logic is certainly undeniable, even in hindsight.

A few weeks went by before my mum had a list of names for me. I laughed out loud when I saw that they all referred to themselves as doctors, and my mum gave me a stern look, one that simultaneously scolded me and let me know that they were, in fact, actually doctors. With the simple raising of her eyebrows and a slight tilt of her neck, she could communicate more than many ever could with words. I logged on to our computer and had a look at some of their websites, and they all seemed like withered old men with spectacles who had read too many textbooks. Again my mother let me know, as she often would, that my commentary was "simply not needed." Finally, I asked her if she really knew who any of these people were. She said that she didn't, but that one of them had worked with her friend's son. I asked who that was, and she pointed him out to me on the list. I said I would go see him.

I guess if I'm being honest, there was a bit of embarrassment about the whole thing. What kind of a fuckup needs to go see a counselor when he's seventeen living in the suburbs? That's what I thought about myself—which was yet another illustration of how kindness and self-empathy were two of my more established character traits. I really couldn't stop being hard on myself about it. I just felt so ungrateful and spoiled and like I was just simply stupid, unable to separate the bigger picture from the small problems of my life. It was all very frustrating, and—despite the fact that no one ever once called me out or challenged me—I got very defensive about it.

Some people say that society puts these ideas in our head that we are supposed to not need any help and that's why people think like this. I don't disagree. All these ideas have to come from somewhere. No one comes out of the womb inherently biased against talking to a counselor. It seems like something we have to pick up somewhere. It's also kind of interesting to think that if at any point my body had started to hurt or I got sick—like how I did in the fourth grade, when I had the experience of a case of diarrhea and vomiting at the same time, leaving a wall in my bathroom irreversibly stained—I would immediately go see a doctor. But seeing a counselor just doesn't seem the same. It seems like if you go to talk to someone about your problems, it's because you're too pathetic to solve them yourself. At least, that's what I thought then.

I hated the fact that I was going to counseling. At least when I went to see Allen York, it was because Jordan had died. That was hard stuff, but it was hard stuff that made some sense. I had lost my best friend. That's going to mess you up. All this other stuff didn't make any sense. I couldn't even really explain it. Here I was, going to counseling because I was depressed and I almost killed myself and I didn't even know why. How embarrassing is that? Who almost kills himself for no reason? Me, I guess. And now I was headed to some stuffy office to talk about it. Maybe I hadn't hit rock bottom yet after all.

THERE IS A part of town far outside of the main core of Victoria that's known as Sooke. It's about a forty-minute drive out of the city depending on traffic and whether any trees have fallen on the road. Trees falling on the road is a thing that really happens in Sooke. As far as places go, Sooke is strikingly gorgeous. There are massive mountains on the side of every road, all overgrown with moss, and ocean views and evergreen trees that seem to come within inches of kissing the clouds. And deep inside Sooke, somewhere where the waves meet the edges of the earth, there is a series of houses tucked away in the quiet, coexisting peacefully in isolation and silence.

In one of these is where I go to talk. It's a looming house with a big backyard and a driveway so steep that it's nearly vertical. As far as places to do counseling go, it's a bit of an untraditional setup really. But it's the best. Something about the long ride into Sooke is calming. Every corner and bend in the asphalt pulls you closer into the quiet, and eventually you're so far into it, you forget what it's like to feel any other way. I feel a lot of peace in Sooke.

If every recovery or restart has a home, this is the one for me. I show up here about once a week and do therapy. It was all a bit of a mystery to me how exactly anyone could partake in such a thing until I started to do it. It seemed ridiculous. You go and talk about your life to a person who doesn't know you and doesn't know your life. The very foundation seems to be built on illusion and foolery. I thought counseling was going to be like going back and living inside all of the stuff inside me that I hate. While it is a little bit like that, with the occasional moment of finding yourself in the middle of all your messiness, having to make your way back out all over again, it's a lot more about figuring out how some of that stuff got there in the first place.

My counselor is a guy by the name of Dr. John Betts. He has a beard and glasses and is always better dressed than I am. A lot of people use the word *wise*. Yet Dr. Betts is the only guy I've ever met who I would deem worthy of that word. He's the smartest person I've ever had a conversation with. It's weird to think about it that way, but it's true. I'm sure there are lots of people with a higher IQ, or who know how to send rockets up in the air or something, but John is the smartest guy I know because he knows about cool things like how to make Ethiopian coffee and hike the mountains parked behind his house, but he knows a whole lot more about how to live life well. He also seems like he has peace of mind. I make note of his peace of mind because it's the thing that will always stand out about him to me. I'm sure he's happy. He definitely seems happy. But I don't notice his happiness as much as I notice how at peace he is with everything. I'm at peace with almost nothing, and so naturally I'm very envious of this.

The first counseling session we ever had together, I sat down in his office and he asked me why I was there. I still had a problem with authority, and so it seemed like a fairly challenging question to open with. I told him that. He said he didn't ask the question to challenge me but rather to figure out how he could best serve me. Standing alone, those words sound a bit like a bad sales pitch for a self-help product. But the feeling behind them made me believe he really did care to help. I hesitated for a second as a few hundred fake answers tried to dance their way from my brain to my tongue. After a deep breath and a pause, I decided to tell him the truth.

"Well . . . I've been super depressed . . . And . . . I almost killed myself a few weeks ago."

I made sure to look him in the eyes when I said it because I didn't want to seem embarrassed—even though I actually was. I'll always remember a certain twitch that took over his pupils as I mentioned suicide. For the tiniest fraction of a second, it looked like a tear was about to surface and swim out of his eyes. Then he swallowed, nodded, and started to make notes. And that's how it all started.

It took John only two meetings to break me down completely. The first hour we spent together was mainly introductory, establishing a background. Things like my name, my family, why I weighed 170 but was six foot six. By the time I was halfway through our next hour together, I was crying so much, I was worried I was going to get dehydrated. Tears flowed out of me effortlessly, as though they had been expecting this moment and were ready to finally be released. Sitting in Sooke, all the answers to all the questions I wanted answers to seemed to show up very clearly. Every cloud of confusion cleared away during those talks, and this penetrating, almost painful perspective of truth showed up, parked itself in my lap, and demanded to be noticed. It can hurt a lot to have that happen. Mostly, though, it feels not unlike the pang of discomfort you feel as a doctor weaves a needle through your arm, stitching your wounds back together, making you whole again.

The best way I can explain my experience with counseling is that I've never once been excited about showing up for a session, and I've never once left a session regretting that I showed up. There are a lot of things in life that leave you with the opposite feeling. Therapy is one thing I've never felt remorse about. I get why it's not totally popular or cool, though. There's no real way to make it sound sexy. It's not something that would make a good bumper sticker, certainly. "I TALKED ABOUT MY PROBLEMS WITH A PROFESSIONAL!" doesn't exactly offer the impression you're a bundle of fun. It's a bunch of work and time and energy, and it will probably make you think things about yourself that you have never thought before, ask questions that you've tried to ignore, and feel things you thought you had already felt. Sometimes, the places your mind will end up going just feel gross, so you want to just run away from that feeling, bury it back under the familiar sand of forgetfulness. But every time you walk out when that hour is up and you step outside and life hits you in the face again, you realize that you're better for it. You're better for knowing who you are rather than pretending to know who you are. John has helped me figure out a few more pieces to the puzzle of who I really am. I'm grateful for that.

THESE DAYS, WHEN I'm in my own head again and overthinking, I try to bring myself back to the feeling of the peace and quiet inside that big house in Sooke. I think about the brown leather chairs and the mahogany side tables and the little desk in the corner. I think about the first few times showing up there and trying to talk through my life. Every hour I've ever spent with John has helped me expand who I am as a person. It's made me more honest, more aware, and a healthier human being.

Counseling has also made me feel like a lucky person. It might sound odd to say that you feel like a lucky person because you pay someone to sit with you for an hour.

But that's not the reason I say it. The reason I feel like a lucky guy is because it has helped me realize that I had a small group of people who were more committed to putting my life back together than I was. I had people believe in me. Take chances on me. Tell me that I was loved, even if I was broken. My mum was the bridge between me and Dr. Betts. She believed in me. And then Dr. Betts was the bridge between me and change. He believed in me. People believed in me when I didn't believe in myself. I think that's a special thing.

As we sat out in the house in Sooke, in those big brown leather chairs, talking about everything I never wanted to talk about, John helped me see that the biggest lie I ever bought into was the one that said I was not worthwhile.

The hard part is, it feels less like a lie and more like the truth when you're seeing life and living it through that lens. When you stop loving yourself, it's impossible— almost insulting—to believe that other people still want to love you. The lie that we don't mean much is all around us. It's not always put so simply, but it's there. It's in the way that cool clothing companies try to make you feel like your life sucks because you're wearing the wrong brands. It's in how we stand in line to take photographs of people we've deemed worthy enough to wait hours for a chance to take photographs with. The walls of the world are painted with words that say we are not good enough. That we don't matter.

I'm not good at math, and my memory isn't much better either, but last I checked, there were around seven billion people on the planet. And you, me, the guy on the street corner—we're just but three of those people. If we listen to the mainstream and if we listen to math, we probably don't matter much. But if you wake up, look around, and realize that your existence, your life, your story, is connecting and colliding with the existences and lives and stories of those around you, maybe math and the mainstream don't paint the whole picture. Maybe we can't be defined by numbers or ads on the back of buses. Maybe we're more than that. I think we are.

There's a sort of secret magic to being alive. There's this thing inside of me that knows I will never be able to fully get to the bottom of just what makes this all so beautiful, yet I'm compelled to continue searching. I feel like a wanderer sometimes, wading my way through the world, wondering at what point it will all start to make sense. But perhaps the purest thing I've ever been able to grasp is that life is not about logic. It's not about getting answers. Life, the very nature of it, defies definitions and doesn't fit into any of our boxes. The visceral experience of being alive—this pounding, penetrating thing that has no explanation—is what makes it so exciting. I used to watch the world spin, wondering when life was going to latch on to me and make me happy. I see now that I had it all wrong. You can't wait. You can't watch. When it comes to being alive, you just have to throw yourself into it, fiercely and fearlessly.

Some say therapy is all about paying money to someone else to get answers you already had in the first place. I think that's pretty funny. But for me, I know it's not true. I found things inside that little room in Sooke that I would never have found inside of my bedroom, eating candy and living in my own head.

Sometimes John frustrated me. His content smile, his perfect sweater vest, and his scientifically brewed coffee with enough caffeine in it to kill an elephant all annoyed me. But mostly he frustrated me because he was a living, breathing, screaming reminder that I could be more. That I could be more than my pain, more than my problems, more than my past. That life could be more. In some ways, like a scared child clinging to his mother's knee, I didn't want to let go of those things. They were nothing good, but they were all I knew. I had spent the majority of my life swimming in that nothingness, and now I was drowning in it. The truth was, I didn't really know who or what I was supposed to be without my blanket of secrecy and shame. I had been eating fear for breakfast, lunch, and dinner. Now I had to wake up and change that. It scared the shit out of me. My issues had become my identity. My pain, my personality. My darkness was all-defining. And yet everything in the world seemed to be shouting at me that this was not true, that this was not a complete picture of me.

While I wanted to believe better things—that I could matter, that I could change—it wasn't easy. When my old ways of thinking would start to creep back up on me, and I felt like I was sliding back down the slippery slope of self-loathing, I would go see John. Those thoughts, the ones that would shout at me about my insignificance and my imperfections, were like anchors in my heart, pulling me further and further down toward my familiar friend despair. I wanted so badly to shake them, and yet they seemed stuck to me. Sitting out in Sooke one day, I bombarded Dr. Betts with my darkest thoughts. He listened to me gently as he always does, and then said something that changed everything.

"Kevin, you know something? You have all the right ideas about life. You probably don't believe that, but you do. But you know what? None of that means anything. You make a better life through example, not opinion. You can't just think things. You gotta actually live them out."

Those words shot out of his mouth and landed in all my messiness like a bullet of brutal truth.

I LEFT SOOKE that day wondering if I could really be someone other than who I had been for the last few years. It seemed like the whole world was conspiring to tell me yes and I was standing there defiantly, shouting back no, clinging to the nothingness with which I had so deeply fallen in love. As I got home, away from the beautiful mountains and the quiet tranquillity, I realized something truer than any thought I'd maybe ever had. The thing about fighting yourself is that when you decide to stop, something really incredible happens: you win.

NOTE TO SELF

Change is never easy but always worth it. Therapy is kind of like the first time you have sex, minus all the stuff that makes sex cool.

9

Dude, Where's My Life?

IT WAS THE dead middle of night and I was wrought with tears, stumbling over myself and my words. I was sitting in the living room in emotional free fall. There is a certain vulnerability you can attain with the person responsible for your being born that is hard to come by in almost any other relationship. I let myself be raw and fully exposed, spilling all my secrets out to my mum. In this moment, time was not important to my mother, neither was the fact she had to work in the morning. Rules, responsibilities, obligations. These were all things that came second to her children. It was admirable and I let her know this by never acknowledging it. Embarrassingly, I just kind of expected it. Even the most devastating, determined love can be taken for granted, I guess.

Sitting there, I was soaked in both my tears and my tremendous angst. My mother, as she calmly drank her tea, was my gentle guide through the whole thing. She held my hand when I would let her, passed me a tissue even though I wouldn't ask for one. She sat there loving me, even when I couldn't love myself.

She is strong and steady: a thousand bricks stacked on top of each other. I envy her sense of self. She knows exactly who she is and desires nothing more. In my raw, angry years, I had seen this as a lack of ambition, but I now realize it for what it is: self-actualization. My mother, in all her light and unyielding love, is exactly who she wants to be. Once I realized this, it became something that has never left me. That's why when there are hard or heavy moments, I turn to her.

She is the greatest listener I know. She will speak only when you have let there be a silence, and she'll let you interrupt her without ever showing the slightest sign that it bothers her. This is not because she is a pushover but because she is nurturing and empathetic. Her love is half compassion and half creativity. Sometimes, on nights like this one, we talk on the couch—the crappy, torn-up green one that I hate—for hours. She gets me to pull things out that I didn't know even existed. While I couldn't admit it then, this was just as much a part of my healing as anything that ever happened out in Sooke. These moments with my mother were a soft place to land. I cherished them but was still too fractured to tell her that.

That particular night, while we talked, it finally came out of me that I was afraid I didn't know who I was. I felt shattered into so many pieces that I didn't know how to be a person anymore. She looked at me in a way which I had seen only a handful of times, a look that was both loving and layered in life experience, and said to me: "The thing about trying to figure out who you are is that it's a big waste of time. You never end up finding yourself, only being a part of the journey which is creating you."

She was right. And slowly, it started sinking in for me that this was what it was going to take for me to live a different life: long talks, tears, and taking the always scary jump of exposing myself and all my fears and quirks to another human being.

QUITE SOME TIME passed before I started to feel like much had really changed in me. It took a lot of hours out in Sooke, sitting across from Dr. Betts, and a lot of hours letting the truth settle into my bones. I have to admit, in some ways it's a lot easier to be depressed than it is to be anything else. You don't really have to do anything when you're depressed. You can just sit and sulk all day, and if you get up and make some food, you've accomplished something. This new feeling—of having to be a functioning person—was nothing like that. It made me kind of miss my old ways, lazily watching the day turn to night and the night turn to morning and my thoughts go from bad to worse. There's something strangely enjoyable about self-destructing. It's almost like you're getting back at the world for all the shit it's ever thrown at you. Truthfully, I missed that sometimes.

I still got sad though. It was infrequent and inconsequential, but it still happened. But there's a big difference between sad and depressed. Enough of a difference that being sad is something to be proud of. Sad is a good thing—a legitimate step up from dim, dysfunctional despair. It means you're still alive and you feel things. So I still got sad from time to time, but it felt a whole lot better than being deeply, darkly depressed, wishing the whole world would collapse upon itself and end our collective misery.

JB IS MY friend. He's seven years older than me, with a bunch of tattoos on his arms and a bunch of interesting, intensely introspective ideas in his head. The reason I really like JB is because he's an honest guy. He's just as fucked up and broken as me, and he doesn't use age as a shield to pretend that he isn't.

His family isn't quite as crazy as mine—at least, not on the outside. His dad is tall and lean, with a smile that stretches so wide across his jaw that it seems like it connects to his ears. He's older, but still rugged and relatable—a handsome guy with a heavy laugh. His mother is short and sincere, and has the ability to fluctuate between serious and silly in a matter of seconds. She is a counselor, a gifted one, and her husband practices law. So JB, as a by-product of his two wonderful parents, holds empathy in one hand and intensity in the other. He and his family grew up in the Yukon, a tiny-ass territory in the north of Canada where people actually fulfill all the common Canadian clichés, complete with igloos and dogsleds. JB grew up in a house with heat and cars and stuff, but that does actually happen in the Yukon. He lived in the capital city, Whitehorse, whose population would be comparable to that of a well-attended community college. It gets dark there early, and sometimes, in the dead of winter, it's dark every hour of the day. When it's like that, JB says you see the most amazing stars. It's their version of the northern lights. It has to be completely black out for you to see them, and then they sneak out from behind the clouds and dance for the world to see. He says it's absolutely spectacular. I've made it a priority to go see them before I die. I'm not much of a fan of stars, but I am a fan of the idea that sometimes life has to go pitch black before you can appreciate the light.

The Yukon is really cold and really desolate and more or less just a terrible place for a child to grow up. JB and his family moved from Whitehorse to Victoria while he was still in high school, which is probably not unlike growing up an atheist and then giving yourself over to God. While

Victoria is no huge city, compared with the Yukon it is overwhelming, alive, crawling with people and possibility.

JB's house was three blocks over from mine, and once we met, down at Maynard Park, we became fast friends. I was still just a kid, scrawny and nervous, and JB was a freshman in college—full of fear and questions about the future. Our friendship formed with a certain ease. The first bridge between us was basketball, and then came our own brokenness. I had never really met anyone, much less someone older than me, who would talk about this sort of stuff. JB was willing to talk and willing to share, and some of the things he would say honestly made me feel better about how badly fucked up I was. As far as qualities to have in a friend go, that one ranks near the top for me.

Mostly, though, as I got older and more passionate about living on the edges of normalcy, we would hang out and smoke weed and pretend to be philosophers.

While I was trying to figure out what life was going to look like, JB was truly there for me. Most people who were older always talked down to me, as if that was what I was hoping for. I don't think anyone likes to be talked down to. At best it's tolerable, and at worst it's demeaning. JB talks to you, never at you, and you have to appreciate that. Sometimes we would talk about what it's like to be a little bit crazy. Not crazy in the sense that you think you can fly or like you should be the leader of a cult or something, but crazy in that you think it's worse to be "normal" than it is to be weird. I used to be so petrified of not being normal. Through many complicated, compassionate conversations with JB, I began to feel like fitting in was as close as you can get to giving up your soul while still remaining alive. It was a change in perspective that made me feel less alone.

For a while, we would go for long nighttime walks in Cadboro Bay and hash out our philosophies. Mostly we talked about our personal problems—for him, post-secondary school; for me, puberty—but invariably, our conversations would come back around to things that were both hard and honest. JB reasoned that fear is the thing that keeps us back and drives us forward at the exact same time. I read a book once where the author said, "We go to war because of fear and we go to spiritual events some-times for the same reason." I passed this along to JB, and an emotionally explosive conversation ensued. JB said that the only time he has ever wanted to fight is when he felt that his words could no longer inflict the same amount of pain that he could if he just curled up his palms. I thought that made a lot of sense. I wondered if maybe hurt and hope are just two different sides of the same coin, one that says we humans want and need to feel alive.

Many nights we spent walking around the empty streets of our sleepy neighborhood, convinced that we were the only people with a pulse who lived there. For some reason, it helped a lot to know that JB wrestled with things, too. Being seven years older than me, he had made seven times as many mistakes; and he was willing to tell me about all of them. For the first time in a long time, I didn't feel totally alone in my tiny little world. Plus, he was less awkward than I was—able to talk to strangers with grace and self-assuredness—and yet he still lived with his parents just a few doors over.

It seemed to me that most people his age tried to stop wondering and start pretending they knew, but JB never did that. He admitted he didn't know anything, and that made me feel better for sharing the same affliction. At least I wasn't alone. Together we became a pair of imperfect people who were stumbling through life. We had a lot of fun doing it. I think if there's a person who can make your pain feel like pleasure, that person should be your friend. We were separated by almost a decade in age and a face full of acne—one that belonged to him, not me—but we were made the same through the struggles we shared.

It's worth noting that JB almost died, too. He went on a trip to Thailand, where he ended up in a crappy hostel with no running water and went into a diabetic low. Only thing was, he had just recently been diagnosed; so he wasn't familiar with its burdens yet. Alone and scared, surrounded only by unfamiliar walls, his whole body just started to shut down on him. He thought he was going to die. He said he was lying in the bathroom, unable to speak, and it felt like his mind was leaving his body. He was just watching it all happen, unable to do anything about it. Sometimes, I have felt that way about my life; memories and moments dangle in front of me, and I am a prisoner to them, not a willing participant.

JB says almost dying gives you the gift of learning what it means to live. It's made me think that maybe some of life's gifts don't come in the box we think they will. Maybe some gifts are too big for a box, too complicated to be conventional. For JB, the new way he's learned to live involves him jabbing a needle into his stomach a few times a day and making sure he has something with sugar in his pockets at all times. He's had to make tiny, subtle adjustments to keep himself on course. It made me wonder what my tiny, subtle adjustments needed to be. The more I thought about it, the more it seemed like maybe it was about finding my own subplot in the much bigger story of life. I think one of the reasons I got depressed a lot was because I was selfish. Not so much selfish in the sense of eating the last slice of pizza without asking, or needing to be noticed all the time; instead, selfish in that I really couldn't see a world bigger than me. If all you can see is yourself, it's pretty easy to live in a dark hole of horribleness. And I don't mean in the sense of the cliché "There are people with bigger problems than you." That's just annoying. It's true, but the reverse is true as well; your problems are bigger than those of some others.

It's not about seeing your problems as small or less important or inferior. It's about waking up to the fact that your life is not the only life there is. I had a really hard time with this one, tougher than it should have been for someone who claims to have half a brain.

I just didn't understand how sometimes people hurt us not because they want to but rather because they don't know how to do anything else. Sometimes others don't give us what we need because they simply don't have it to give. And sometimes, even when all you can see is how you're being let down, you're forgetting that you should be more focused on how you can help someone else up.

If the whole world revolves around you, eventually that's going to make you feel like you're not a very good person. Otherwise, all people would treat you well or better. They don't; often they can't. People can only love you as much as they love themselves. Sometimes you have to live with that. Even when it hurts your heart, and even when it conflicts with your beliefs about what should be.

If I can be honest, my depressed days are mostly a mixture of feeling the bruises of the world and missing its beauty. That's okay, too. I don't expect myself or anyone for that matter to be unfettered by the world around us. If you are, it's because you're emotionally unavailable, not because you're enlightened. Sometimes you have to live outside your own bubble and get lost somewhere in the big picture.

The truth, the one that kept sneaking up on me during those sleepless nights wandering around the streets of Cadboro Bay, is this: You are alive. You are here. You have two hands and two eyes and two ears and a head and a heart. You can make people cry. You can make people smile. You can build big things that make people stop and wonder. Or you can break things that others have built. The choices are all yours. But you are not the big story. You're just selfish if you think so. Life is the big story. You are merely a subplot. What you do with that subplot is up to you.

All of this hit me in a way that was both devastating and defiantly beautiful.

NOTE TO SELF

Repeat after me: I am not the most important thing in the world. I am not the most important thing in the world. But that doesn't make me unimportant. It just makes me human.

10

Thinking Better Thoughts

OUR WHOLE LIVES everyone tells us to grow up and be happy. The more I think about it, the less it seems like a very good idea. Certainly, I think you can experience happiness. But happy is sort of like the wind; you can never tell what direction it's coming from or how much longer it's going to keep on coming. I think "Be happy" is bad advice. Certainly, it made my life a bit of a wreck.

I think what we really want is much more complex than being happy. I think we want meaning. Happiness is like a bong hit. Meaning is like being plugged in to something pure; it's strong, enduring, a constant connection to something more. We need meaning. The thing about it, though, is there is really only one road to travel to find it. That road is filled with rocks and bumps and dead ends and disappointments and despair. There's no road map, no instruction book. No one who can tell you whether to turn right or left. You just show up and feel your way through the whole thing. You hurry up and scrape your knee. And when you fall, you find a reason, any reason you can, to get back up.

PERHAPS THE TRUTH is simply that my life wasn't as bad as what I had created in my head. I helped make the glass half empty when it could have been half full. After a while, not being happy or not being whole becomes its own addiction. Being a mess is just who you are somehow. It's nothing, but you wouldn't know what to do without that nothingness. It's what keeps you going. Your darkness and despair become something to think about and obsess over. All the things that hurt us are also things I allowed myself to become obsessed about. All the little imperfections, the little jagged edges, the little pieces of brokenness, were lying on the floor of my life, and I just kept picking them back up and letting them cut me.

I guess that it's easier to believe you're broken and defective than to believe anything else. If you believe you're a fuckup, all the pressure falls off of you. In the most twisted sense, being a fuckup gives you freedom. The freedom to not care. The freedom to be selfish. The freedom to become poisonous and not to change.

When you stop believing those things about yourself,

you actually lose that freedom. You have to become a better person. You have to stop selling yourself short. You have to stop hurting people and hiding behind the excuse that you are flawed. You have to stop using the blanket of being a fuckup and expose yourself. Get naked. When you do that, when you finally find the will to do that, you discover that your life has limits. I used to think those limits were the enemy, that they were confining walls that would close in upon me and crush me. Now I see that they're actually the opposite. They empower and embolden. We need boundaries to find balance. We need limits, because otherwise we have nothing to keep life and all its choices in check. Turns out, boundaries aren't the enemy. Bad beliefs are.

The thing that finally gave me freedom, and took me forever to figure out, is you need to separate your issues from your identity. Your pain is not your personality. Your struggle is not a summation of your soul. But I didn't know that back then. I thought we were our mistakes. I thought our cuts were supposed to be our character. They're not, though. Imperfections are neither good nor bad; they just are. The same way trees just are or rocks just are. They simply exist. Any meaning we choose to attach to a thing, a thought, a defect, a pain, an imperfection, we are choosing to attach to it because of our own beliefs. Often because of our own bullshit. We are always telling a story. We're always forging meaning, trying to figure our way out of our mess. Sometimes we're just doing it wrong.

Sometimes we're just telling the wrong story.

My childhood was a lot better than I could ever give it credit for while I was growing up. It taught me everything I ever needed to know, I think. How to do things well and how to mess things up and how to love people and how to let people love you back. But I also was selfish. I was self-obsessed. I cared about pleasure first and avoiding pain second. I wanted the world to wake up and give itself to me in its entirety. I didn't know that the only way I would ever be happy was if I woke up and tried to give something to the world.

I was waiting for people to love me in ways that matched this ridiculous, irrational expectation I had created, not realizing no one could ever live up to the fantasy. I didn't know that if I wanted to feel love, I should try to hand it to someone rather than hoard it for myself. I grew up and never knew that I needed to stop waiting for life to find me and instead run outside and find life.

I THINK LIFE is what happens when your plans fall apart and circumstances collide with your character. That's really it, from what I can see. Very little of what we spend time planning or worrying about ever actually happens. We wait all week for the weekend and wait all year for summer and wait all our life for love, and doing this almost always lets us down. We sit stoically in patience and in pride, and then we get disappointed. Like a spilled can of paint, life's imperfections bleed into our lives, and sometimes we wear that mess all over ourselves.

Some days, a lot of days, actually, I feel like I've got one rope on my left arm trying to pull me into the past and one rope on my right arm trying to drag me into the future, and I'm standing there trying not to get split in half. I resent yesterday and fear tomorrow and in doing so end up missing today.

It's hard to quiet the plaguing voice of pessimism. It's not unlike having the world's worst friend live inside your head all day. Every time you see a sunrise or a wave crash atop a rock, he shows up and reminds you about that time you got caught masturbating. And no matter how much you tell your friend to fuck off, he just keeps hanging around. Silently standing in the shadows until it's time to take a moment of your life and suck all the joy right out of it.

Most of my problems are tied to this kind of thinking, constantly putting me in the middle of two worlds well beyond my control. Most of our pain is in the past, and most of our torturous anxiety is in tomorrow. Very few things are tearing us up today, other than our thoughts about what's behind or in front of us. It's a weird paradox. I guess this seems too simple to be the answer. I want it to be bigger than this and more mysterious. There's something about angst and a longing for more that the movies try to make sexy. As if it's somehow artistic or poetic to live a life of pain. But for me, it's never been like that. It's always been like a cut that I want badly to heal but that never really does.

I WONDERED FOR a long time whether or not living in the moment is a way of ignorance being bliss. It seemed that way for a little while. There was this part of me that felt guilty about feeling good because I was ignoring the bad. I'm a bit of a truth addict, sometimes to a fault. If it's true and it happened, I want to live in my own head about it, obsessing over every dirty detail, good or bad. While it seems like there's an intellectual dignity to that, as if forcing yourself to suffer is somehow "smart," it's a really shitty way to live.

Once I went on a walk to a part of a nearby beach called Smuggler's Cove. I'm not really sure why they call it that, but I've turned it into quite the fantasy in my own head, with mustached gangsters during Prohibition unloading barrels of whiskey and holding machine guns. Probably none of that happened, but if you can make yourself believe it did, the little plot of sand sitting out there on the edges of Cadboro Bay is suddenly that much more exciting. So I went on a walk to Smuggler's Cove. If I just walked in a straight line from my house, it would take me less than ten minutes. But bored by repetition and routine, I wanted to try a new way and approach it from the other side. Luckily, there was a small map near Maynard Park that showed a few different routes. Unluckily, my map-reading skills are similar to my second-language skills, and by that I mean they don't exist. So I got terribly lost and ended up on the completely wrong side of the beach. The other side of the beach is rocky and hard to navigate and much less beautiful. I was both pissed and slightly embarrassed that I had ended up there. But I took a breath, realized I was still alive, that all was not lost, and decided to just start again. Eventually I made it.

Later, I wondered why it was so easy for me to do that, breathe and redirect, and why I couldn't do that in my life. I think every time I've ever been depressed, it's because I'm standing on the wrong side of the beach, looking across the water, pissed off that I ever ended up here. In reality, I'm not on the crappy side of the beach and I'm not even headed toward it; I'm just thinking about it. And you know what? It kind of ruins the view. It kind of ruins your life.

I used to think that focusing on the here and now was just a cute way of ignoring life. Now I see it's the opposite: the here and now is life. Everything else is just self-talk. I guess part of the reason this is hard to handle is we're kind of told to look forward to things. To get excited about Christmas and birthdays and vacations and what's going to happen when everything transforms into a whirlwind of wonder and whimsy. But that's not really life. Life is just this moment. Maybe the moment isn't all that incredible, but maybe it doesn't have to be either. Maybe we need to just sit still sometimes and shut up, so we don't become overwhelmed by how everything we see in our human existence is piercingly epic and void of rational explanation.

The thing is, if we take away the option to rewind or project forward, all we're left with is what we do and who we are. The happiness and the joy have to come from what we're doing right here, right now. And that's a lot of pressure for a person. The day I took ownership of my experiences, I was shaken and scared. Because at first, being responsible for your own life feels like a burden. But then you realize it's actually freedom. The freedom to finally stop assigning blame, to stop wondering what is waiting for you. The freedom to figure life out on your terms, not anyone else's.

Suddenly, lingering inside me was the quiet belief that maybe I was going to be okay. It was a quiet, comforting thought that I turned to more and more. For the first time, I stopped wondering if I was normal. Now, I knew there was no such thing. Everyone has his or her own idea of "normal." But it's likely just a fantasyland of normal. There is no real normal. Normal is a moving, flickering target that's best not to aim at. I can finally accept that in a way that is both freeing and scary.

To denounce normal was one thing. But to actually stop holding myself to invisible standards was another. The fact that I had to own up to being responsible for myself was a harsh realization. When you're a kid fully committed to being a fuckup, you're so lost in self-loathing that you don't realize how easy it is to continue that way. To be a fuckup is to not care. To purposefully and persistently fight against reaching your own potential. When you want to change, though, you have to care.

Of all the epiphanies I had, this one was the hardest. I could no longer be the kid who didn't care about himself or anyone else. I couldn't steep in the simplicity of being broken. I was now someone who had something to care about, to strive after: being better, living better.

Occasionally, when I sit at Smuggler's Cove and watch the waves greet the sand, surfers come by. Usually they're by themselves with a wetsuit, a small board, and big eyes as companions. They watch the water for a while, and I watch them. In all these years, I've noticed something: no one has ever once caught a wave standing on the shore. They all go out there and meet adventure in the middle. You can't just stand and watch. You need to shut up and paddle. A lot of guys get knocked off their boards. The great ones seem to take that as encouragement that they're chasing the right waves. And they just keep on chasing them. There's something true and right about that. I don't surf and I don't own a wetsuit, but I want to own that kind of perspective about life. Right now, I feel like, at best, I'm renting it.

I hope one day I'll have my name all over it.

NOTE TO SELF

Good or bad, we're all living a story. The thing about stories is, the good ones never end the way they started.

Epilogue

RIGHT AS I got near to the end of writing this book, I hit what I can only describe as a massive mountain of an emotional roadblock. I felt exhausted and tired and like I was pointlessly pursuing a story I couldn't make sense out of. As much as I had found some meaning in my life, and had seen how some of my pain helped to shape my perspective, I didn't get what it was all for. It seemed like so much of my life had been falling down, getting back up, and falling down again. For about as long as I can remember, I've been obsessed with stories. I love the raw, real, imperfect ones. I wanted my story to feel as good as the stories I used to read and watch. To be completely honest, it just felt like my story sucked. There were a few days of brutal hit-head-into-wall-and-cry days, and I really, truly wondered if I was going to be able to finish this project.

When I get this far inside my own head, usually I can remind myself to just call a couple of people who I care about and they'll verbally slap me around or support me; I'll sleep it off, wake up, and everything is fine again. So I picked up the phone and went for some dinners and got lost in conversations, and something strange happened: nothing got better. Instead of finding clarity, it seemed like I only encountered more chaos. So I did what (in my own imagination) any self-respecting writer would do; I had three glasses of wine and went to bed. My sleep came slowly and with a lot of convincing I deserved it, but eventually my exhaustion outweighed my self-shaming and I drifted off. Right before I fully went out, I remembered I hadn't set my alarm. Too tired to move, I didn't do anything about it. Turns out, I wouldn't need that alarm.

At 2:33 in the morning, I had the pure pleasure of awaking to the blaring, belligerent noise of the fire alarm inside my condo going off. It was so insanely loud, I screamed out, "What the FUCK?!" and was unable to hear my own profanity; this was both a pleasant surprise and a shockingly scary moment at the same time. Frantically, as well as nakedly, I sprinted all over my condo trying to turn off each of my six fire alarms. What anyone needs six alarms in one apartment for is far beyond me. Maybe the last guy who lived here was deaf or something. Running around half awake, half still somewhere in deep slumber, I was convinced one of the incenses that I burn—to pretend I'm an enlightened person, of course—had set off the alarm and that I was subsequently waking up the entire world with my sham spirituality. As I slipped and fell all over my hardwood floor in desperate pursuit of silence, I realized that it wasn't just my alarm going off. It was every alarm in the building. And then it happened: I smelled the smoke. It snuck in under the door like a pesky rodent, bringing with it primal fear.

I live on the fourth floor and immediately felt my heart rate increase to a speed that I would only expect to see from a race car driver doing cocaine. I had been awake for all of thirty-nine seconds, and so far I had realized:

1. There's a fire.
2. There's a fire.
3. I'm naked.
4. There's a fire.
5. I'm going to have to jump off my balcony, into the flower garden below.
6. My eulogy is going to read, "He died as he lived, naked and scared."

I started to panic. In a rush, I threw on sweatpants—backward, no less—and a T-shirt: appropriate dress for midwinter. I scrambled to find my keys, as, even though the entire building was about to burn down, I didn't want to break routine. And then I started to freak the fuck out.

Uncontrollably, I started yelling: "GET OUTSIDE, YOU IDIOT!" I kept repeating this, screaming at no one in particular. "GET OUTSIDE! GET OUTSIDE! DO NOT STAY HERE!"

I sprinted out the door, ready to see flames and face my imminent moment of truth. As I ran down the stairs, thoughts popped into my mind.

You're fucked!

You're really fucked!

My pants are on backward!

No one is ever going to read my book!

And then it hit me. I realized I was absolutely petrified of dying. I was scared to the bone of never seeing my mum again, and never getting to write another word, or laugh or cry or have another night with my best friends where we stay up so late it becomes early morning. I was so scared to die, I didn't know what to do.

I say all this because this is to date the proudest moment of my life. I lived a lot of my life hoping for a way out. Hoping for an early ending. And I almost gave myself that exit. And that night, running out of my building wearing a T-shirt, backward sweatpants, and unfiltered fear, I realized just how far I had come. I'm someone who loves life now. I know that's so fucking cheesy to say, but I do. I really love life. I'm excited for it. I can't wait to keep on living it. And I realize that's why, unbeknownst to me, I kept waking up each day, slaving away at this book, working on a project that required only words, and yet I could never find any to describe it.

I wrote this book as an invitation to a better life for anyone who has been where I've been. It's for anyone who has ever felt like the rough edges of life were piercing into their skin and scraping against their soul and making continued existence seem empty. I wrote this book because I know what it's like to feel broken and defective.

Turns out, some lady was cooking bacon and started a stove fire. They put it out in about five minutes and everything was fine. Everyone walked back into our building, back into our little boxes and our little lives. I realized then that I had changed. I was no longer a prisoner to my pain.

I know what it's like to want to die. And now I can say I honestly know what it means to want to live.

Acknowledgments

To the reader, thank you so much for taking the time to get lost in these pages. I spend my life trying to find the right words, and yet I can't find any to express just how grateful I am for that. I hope we get to meet someday.

To my mum, thanks for caring about a kid as messed up as I once was. I don't know how you did it, but I sure am grateful you did. You never doubted me or judged me. What a special gift. I love you.

To my sister, thanks for giving me my first real journal all those years back. If it had come from anyone else, it would have been just a leather notebook. But since it came from you, it inspired me to do what I do today. Thank you.

To my friends, for tricking me into believing I could actually finish this thing and then making sure that I did.

To Heather Jackson, for taking a chance on a teenage

kid from Canada who barely kept up with his own blog. Thanks for encouraging me to bleed onto the page and to do work that matters. Hopefully, I didn't let you down.

To AP, for always making me laugh and reminding me that I spend too much time staring at my computer.

To Josh Shipp, you're my friend and mentor. Thank you for helping me understand one of the most crucial life lessons I've ever acquired: what got you here won't get you there. I owe you one.

To Jed Wallace, thank you for keeping me sane through this whole thing. I'll never forget your texts of encouragement and hilarity. You're a true class act in a business that breeds the opposite. But more than anything, your story inspires me. You are everything that they say an ex-addict can't be. I'm proud to know you.

To Mr. Szatsmary, thanks for telling me I could be a writer. Your English class was the first place I ever learned to take my work seriously. Ever since then I've been trying to write something that I think will make you proud. I'm not sure if that will ever happen, but I'm gonna keep on trying.

To JB, at the risk of sounding outrageously lame, you've always kept it real. I appreciate you being who you are. Thank you for all the powerful conversations over the years. They have put me on a path to a life lived more positively. I'm grateful for that.

To Allen York, you saved my life. You spoke truth even

when it was tough to do, and you cared about me even when I couldn't care about myself. Thank you. I would not be here without you, and I mean that in the literal sense. The work you've spent your life doing matters in the most meaningful of ways. On behalf of myself and every kid you've ever helped: thank you.

To Dr. Betts, you have given me perspective on my pain that I never thought possible. You are a kind and gentle soul, and I'm thankful you decided to dedicate your life to doing what you do. Indeed, it has changed my life—and that of so many others—for the better. This book would never have made it to print if it weren't for your challenging words to "stop believing my own bullshit." Thank you.

To Taylor Conroy, thank you for being there for me in one of the most challenging times of my life. Your perspective and input guided me through a season when I felt impossibly stuck in my own questions. I will never forget that. You are an unbelievable example of grace. Thank you.

To Jamie Tworkowski, thanks for being someone who lives a great story. You are an example of both honesty and humility. Put plain and simple: you inspire me. Your work has saved lives and given hope to so many. That is the largest of gifts. Thank you for reminding me to get up every day and do important things and say stuff that I believe. One day I will learn to surf and move to Florida. I promise.

To Simon Whitfield, you came and spoke at my elementary school when I was just a little kid. Now that I'm a big kid, I feel privileged to know you. You will never know just how much hope it gave me to see someone from our little town do something on the world stage. A simple note you sent ended up changing my career, but more than anything, your example of how to pursue excellence ended up changing my life. Thank you.

To Clara Hughes, thank you for showing me what hard work looks like. I will never be able to forget our time together on the road. You are not only a world-class athlete but also a world-class human being. Thank you for always proving the doubters wrong. Every day I get up and try to live my day with purpose because that's what you told me to do. Thank you for saying things that everyone needs to hear. It's what you do best.

To Loring Phinney, thanks for taking a chance on a young guy with no media training to be the national spokesperson of a media campaign. It sounds ridiculous— and it probably is—but somehow we make it work. I appreciate you so much. You have a heart for this stuff, and it shows. I'll never forget the day that you, Steve, and I spent in North Bay, Ontario. It changed my life. Thank you.

To my uncle John, thank you for your wisdom and your mentorship. We have the smallest family in the world, but it doesn't matter. I'm so grateful for all your help over the years. You've always spoken the truth to me, and I can't tell you how much I appreciate it. Thank you for being on my team.

And last, to Jordan McGregor: you were a son, a brother, and my best friend. You had infinite patience and unyielding love and were the most authentic person I ever met. You taught me how to live life without fear. That's something that I carry with me every single day. I can't explain how much I miss you. Life has forever left me speechless, since the day I found out you left us. You were unbounded love. You would light up the world if you were still around. I think about you all the time, man. Maybe they can take your life, but they sure can't take your light. You are one of one. We all miss you very much. May you rest in peace, my friend.

One More Note to the Reader

This book was really hard for me to write. The reason being, I think, that so much of what I wrote about is heavy, messy stuff. Stuff like depression and suicide. While I'm grateful for how my pain has shaped my perspective, it wasn't easy to make it to this point. And the truth is, I didn't do it alone. Far from it. I had a small group of people who cared more about my life than I did at the time. They put the pieces back together for me, when I was too weak to do so myself. Every day I feel grateful for that.

I say all of that to say this: if you're struggling, ask for help. Please, ask for help. Ignore your pride and invite people into your problems. If it wasn't for counseling and having conversations about the things I was wrestling with inside, I'm not sure I would be here.

That's why I want to recommend a resource to you, the

reader. It's a nonprofit called To Write Love on Her Arms. My friend Jamie founded it as a simple attempt to help one friend pay for her recovery. Now it has literally helped millions of people struggling with depression, addiction, self-harm, and suicide. If anything in these pages has hit home with you, or if you feel like you're struggling, please consider visiting the website. They have given so many people hope and pointed even more toward help. I promise you will be inspired. This is their life's work and what they do best.

Whether you use it today, tomorrow, or ten years from now or you simply suggest it to a friend, know that there is a group of people out there who care about you and your story. I'm proud to know them, call them friends, and get to see firsthand how their work is transforming the world.

TWLOHA.com